MW00474304

How to
Make Melt & Pour Soap Base From Scratch

A Beginner's Guide to Melt & Pour Soap Base Manufacturing

By Kayla Fioravanti, R.A.
Certified and Registered Aromatherapist, Cosmetic Formulator

Other Books by Kayla
The Art, Science and Business of Aromatherapy,
Your Guide for Personal Aromatherapy and Entrepreneurship

DIY Kitchen Chemistry, Simple Homemade Bath & Body Projects

Coming Soon!
When I was Young I Flew the Sun as a Kite

Puffy and Blue

Selah Press

Reviews

"The book, "How to Make Melt and Pour Soap Base from Scratch" is one the soapmaking industry has long been clamoring for. Noted aromatherapist, Kayla Fioravanti, has done her research, spent countless hours in the lab formulating and is now sharing her information with the soapmaking world. And we are all the better for it. For anyone who has wondered, "Just how is melt and pour made?" to the experienced soapmaker who wants to control their own ingredients and supply chain, this book has something in it for everyone.

In addition to Melt and Pour formulas, step by step instructions and a detailed ingredient discussion, this book also addresses important issues such as: "How do I turn this hobby into a business?" and "What sort of manufacturing practices should I be following when I make this soap?" If you're curious about how Melt and Pour soap is made or just want to learn a new craft, this book is for you."
Anne-Marie Faiola, The Soap Queen

"Kayla's book, "How to Make Melt & Pour Soap Base From Scratch", bridges a gap in handcrafted soapmaking literature, giving those who tend toward the do-it-yourself philosophy a much-needed guide for making melt & pour soap. The notes on what has (and hasn't) worked in her formulating experience will prove invaluable to those who want to take their melt & pour soapmaking to the next level. Any soapmaker seeking to expand their soapmaking horizons will benefit from not only the technical details contained in the book, but also from Kayla's insights into her personal journey and her advice."
Marie Gale, Author of Soap & Cosmetic Labeling

"Whether you are just starting out in the cosmetics field, or you are a seasoned veteran who wants to more fully understand the melt & pour soapmaking process, "How to Make Melt & Pour Soap Base From Scratch" delivers everything you need to fully embrace the topic. From assembling the ingredients and making the soap, to properly labeling it to comply with regulatory requirements, you'll benefit from the easy, breezy style Kayla is known for. It's like she's standing right next to you every step of the way. This book is destined to be a classic reference in the cosmetic industry for decades to come, and I highly recommend it!"
Donna Maria Coles Johnson, Founder & CEO, INDIE Beauty Network

"Kayla has used her 13 years in the cosmetic industry to produce a book that is well written, in terms that a layman could begin manufacturing Melt and Pour soap today. Kayla has provided all aspects required to have or create a successful business in the cosmetic industry. More importantly, Kayla has shown the reader what is required of a manufacturer, and the facts surrounding ingredients, regulations, safety and guidelines."
Lisa M. Rodgers, Co-Founder of Personal Care Truth

"Kayla continually astounds me with her breadth of knowledge and, in particular, her unique gift for distilling what is often very technical scientific information down to its essence, making it accessible for formulator on every level. Her knowledge, passion and commitment to this industry is one of our most valuable assets. This book does not disappoint and is certain to become an invaluable guide the reader will reach for again and again. Succinct, well organized and brimming with valuable information."
Lela Rain Barker, Founder & Creative Director Bella Luccè

How to Make Melt & Pour Soap Base from Scratch
A Beginner's Guide to Melt & Pour Soap Base manufacturing

By Kayla Fioravanti, R.A., Cosmetic Formulator

Editing by Dana Brown and Lesley Anne Craig

Cover and Text Design by Alex Badcock

Copyright © 2011 by Kayla Fioravanti

ISBN-13: 978-0615481111

Printed in the United States of America

Published by
Selah Press

Notice of Rights
All rights reserved. No part of this book may be reproduced or transmitted in any form by any means, electronic, mechanical, photocopy, recording or other without the prior written permission of the publisher. For information on getting permission for reprints and excerpts, contact permissions@kaylafioravanti.com

Notice of Liability
The author has made every effort possible to check and ensure the accuracy of the information and recipes presented in this book. However, the information herein is sold without warranty, either express or implied. Neither the author, publisher nor any dealer or distributor will be held liable for any damages caused either directly or indirectly by the instructions, recipes or information contained in this book.

Errors
To report any errors in this book, please send a note to:
errors@kaylafioravanti.com

Author Website
www.kaylafioravanti.com

Dedication

This book is dedicated to my mother, Helen "Kelley" Mohs, who taught me how to live and die with grace, creativity and dignity. It was my honor to be at her side as she surrendered her 44 year fight to survive.

Upon Goodbye

It is nearly impossible
to think of you in the past tense.
Your life is colorfully woven into the fabric of ours.
I know you are gone,
I saw you leave,
but in my memory you are vividly alive,
with your mischievous smile
teasing the corners of your mouth.

Saying "she was…"
doesn't fit comfortably on my tongue yet
because you left bold strokes upon my life.

I see you "alive" all around me.
You live in the impression
you left upon your grandchildren.
Your life is etched in the laugh lines
worn deeply into my father's face from a lifetime
of joy shared with "the love of his life."
I see you in the bold brush strokes you left on canvas
and the lives you touched.
I can hear you in the language of my motherhood
and the dialect of my life.

I feel your strength that you wove deep
into the hearts of my brother and me
because you always knew
you would leave us too soon.

Death may have taken you,
but what you left behind
Will echo in our lives
for generations to come.

Kayla Fioravanti to Mom
Helen "Kelley" Mohs :: October 29, 1941 to February 9, 2011

Acknowledgements

I am often asked, "Kayla, how do you do it all?" The answer: It takes a village. I don't often have an opportunity to thank my village publicly, so please indulge my grateful praises for a moment.

My husband Dennis is the village leader in my life. I followed him here, and I'd follow him anywhere. His business vision is always bold, inspiring and insightful. It can also be scary. He sees what can be and isn't afraid to lead the way there. I've learned not to hold him back but to buckle in for the ride because where he goes I will go---and it will be a grand adventure. My kids inspire me every day to live up to the elevated status they give me. Thank you to Keegan, Selah and Caiden for understanding when I tell them, "Mommy is focusing right now." They make entrepreneurship worth the blood, sweat, tears and prayers. (A special shout out to Miss Dana for standing in the gap when I travel or can't be there with them.)

I wouldn't be where I am today without the guidance and support of my parents. Growing up in their home was a special privilege. They fed and nurtured my creativity, inquisitive mind and independence. They also taught me by example about love, commitment, hard work and marriage.

Special thanks to my editors Dana Brown and Lesley Anne Craig for cleaning up my grammar. Many thanks to Marie Gale, Donna Maria Coles Johnson, Steven Borden, Kathy Steinbock and Diane Humke for your different perspectives. As well as my R&D Team Ryan Mader, Adam Pennington, and Kyle Allen. Everyone gave me incredible insight that helped shape this book. And a special shout out to Lisa Rodgers, Lela Barker and Anne-Marie Faiola for your words of praise. Thanks David Sanford of Credo Communications for making a mole hill out of mountain by sharing his publishing knowledge.

I am especially blessed to be supported by a great team at Essential Wholesale. Ryan Mader gave me priceless R&D assistance by making some of the early batches of these recipes. I could not have taken the time to write this book without Ryan's leadership in the R&D Lab. I have left a lot of balls in the air at Essential Wholesale during these first few months of 2011. I am blessed to have a great team at Essential Wholesale. I want to call out Essential Wholesale leadership team Laura Badcock, Barry Weinmann, Diane Humke and Alex Badcock for consistently going above and beyond the call of duty. With the support of my village I was able to focus and accomplish what needed to be done.

I am also thankful for our Essential Wholesale customers for giving us the privilege of being a part of their dreams. We never could have reached for our dreams without you. Last, but most importantly, I am eternally grateful for my Creator and Savior Jesus.

Table of Contents

About the Author

Kayla is a Certified, ARC Registered Aromatherapist and the co-Founder and Chief Formulator for Essential Wholesale and its lab division Essential Labs. Wife and mother of three, she runs her company along with her husband Dennis. In 1998, Kayla started creating products in her kitchen using essential oils. They turned the profit from their first batch of products into more supplies, have repeated the process over and over again to remain a debt free company.

In 2000 they started an all natural aromatherapy based Home Party Plan. In 2002, they changed their business plan and became the distribution and manufacturing company, Essential Wholesale. This was followed by the addition of Essential Labs in 2005. The initial $50 investment from their home kitchen, combined with blood, sweat and prayers, has now become a multi-million dollar organically certified and FDA compliant company.

Kayla is the go-to industry specialist for formulating and supplying information on aromatherapy, natural, organic and pure cosmetics and personal care items. She formulates thousands of products including: mineral make up, skin care, body care and products for bath, spa, hair, baby, pets, aroma and much more. Through her lab division, Essential Labs, Kayla formulates private label personal care products for all size businesses worldwide.

Kayla can be found on YouTube in the Essential Wholesale series Kitchen Chemistry with Kayla where she teaches a variety of Do It Yourself (DIY) recipes. Kayla's articles and advice can be found in hundreds of publications including: Dermascope, Les Nouvelles Esthetique, Global Cosmetic Industry (GCI), Saponifier, NAHA, Real Simple, Self, Prevention, Good Housekeeping, Home Business, Women Entrepreneur, Elle, Redbook, InStyle, Woman's World and Essential Wholesale's educational arm the Essential U blog. She wrote a chapter in the book Millionaire Mom, The Art of Raising a Business and a Family at the Same Time by Joyce Bone. Kayla has been a guest on Millionaire Moms Radio, Organic Beauty Radio, Indie Radio, KPDQ Northwest Showcase, Good Day Oregon, 104.1 The Fish and more.

Kayla is the driving force behind the Essential U blog, an educational center for aromatherapy, cosmetics, industry standards and business ownership. She shares her knowledge as an expert on the Personal Care Truth, Information Based on Scientific Facts website because of her passion to spread science based factual information about cosmetics and the personal care industry. Kayla has been an outspoken advocate for small business owners in the halls of Congress. One of her goals is to help protect small businesses from regulatory interference which may hamper the pursuit of the American dream.

Introduction

This book is unique. It is written from the perspective of a Cosmetic Formulator on the production of the popular cosmetic base known as, Melt and Pour Soap. The craft market is flooded with books on how to melt, mold, mix, design and otherwise create the finished Melt and Pour Soap bars. This book teaches you how to make that Melt and Pour Soap base from scratch. I'm not going to cover all the ways you can create finished products from the Melt and Pour Soap base. A quick search on Amazon or on the internet will turn up books, tutorials and videos on how to craft all of those; instead I will teach you to manufacture Melt and Pour Soap base from scratch and thereby cut out the middle man and better manage your controls.

This book will give you a clean definition of true soap versus Melt and Pour Soap. I will also give you guidance on how, as a small home based business, you can follow the regulations, labeling laws and industry standards for selling soap and cosmetics.

My entire journey into the cosmetic industry started with Melt and Pour Soap shortly after I discovered aromatherapy. The roots of our business, Essential Wholesale, all started in December of 1998. My husband, Dennis, was in college and working full-time. I was a stay at home mom with a six-year old and one on the way. Since we were too broke to buy Christmas presents that year, we decided to make gifts for friends and family. I had a one ounce bottle of tea tree essential oil in my kitchen cabinet left over from the case of ringworm our son, Keegan, had the previous July. I decided to find a way to incorporate that bottle of tea tree in our Christmas gifts because, after all, I already had a bottle on hand.

Before my son's ringworm I wasn't familiar with aromatherapy. His case was persistent and I had already tried all the over-the-counter drugs and prescription drugs for ringworm. I headed to the health food store to read their books in search of a cure. We were living in a small town in Oklahoma at the time and the local health food store was tiny and empty. The clerk was bored so she joined me in my search for a natural cure for ringworm. Every book we picked up referenced tea tree essential oil as the most effective cure for ringworm. I took the plunge and invested $11.00 retail cost to buy an ounce of tea tree essential oil.

Much to my surprise, within three days my son's ringworm was completely cured. Since I had always used unscented products because of the allergic reactions I had to chemical fragrance oils, I had assumed that I would be allergic to the tea tree essential oil as well. Instead I discovered it wasn't the essential oils extracted directly from a plant source that caused my allergies, but I was only allergic to fragrance oils that were synthetically manufactured.

Tea tree essential oil opened up a whole new world for me. I was so excited that I spent August through December with my nose in one aromatherapy book after another. I was completely fascinated by this thing called aromatherapy. I checked out piles of books at the library until I had read everything I could find on the subject. Even though we couldn't afford to buy aromatherapy books or any other essential oils, my head was full of new and fascinating knowledge.

The natural progression of my aromatherapy fascination was to use the tea tree essential oil to make Christmas gifts that year. I decided to use Melt and Pour Soap that I found at my local craft store to make colorful and fun Christmas gifts. My husband saw the business potential of these soaps and created re-order forms to go with the Christmas gifts (tacky, I know). It turns out that our friends and family liked our soaps. They bought more and told their friends and families about our mail-order soap business that was starting to blossom.

Our little business venture kept growing and expanding into other products and business models along the way. When I really started researching the ingredients used in the Melt and Pour Soap base I discovered it wasn't completely natural after all. I ventured into handcrafted soaps, but found what I really loved was the creativity and instant results of Melt and Pour Soap. In addition, I was having no allergic reaction to the Melt and Pour soap base and neither were my customers.

As our business expanded we began to focus on natural cosmetics and personal care products. However, I never lost my curiosity and fascination with Melt and Pour Soap. Over the years we moved from our home kitchenette to a 600 square foot space, to a 2500 square foot building, to a 10,000 square foot space in a bigger building, and from there we have expanded into 30,000 square feet of that same building. In 2011 our business will be moving to an even larger 58,000 square foot building.

Our relationship with Melt and Pour Soap changed over the years. At first we sold retail customized Melt and Pour Soaps. We then bought and sold the company Critter Soaps. Later we sold thousands of pounds worth of wholesale Melt and Pour Soap base and eventually discontinued selling Melt and Pour Soap because the price kept rising. At the time Melt and Pour Soap was the only cosmetic base we sold that we didn't manufacture ourselves. It simply didn't make sense to wholesale someone else's base when our business model had changed to selling only the bases we manufactured ourselves.

It was at this point in our business that I decided it was time to formulate our own Melt and Pour Soap ourselves. It didn't take long to have working formulas, but at that moment we were using up every inch of space in our 30,000 square foot building. We were bursting at the seams and couldn't accommodate the manufacturing and cooling of the Melt and Pour Soap Base in bulk. Our space was so tight we couldn't possibly cool an 8,000 lb batch of Melt and Pour Soap base into multiple 1 lb, 20 lb and 40 lb blocks to sell in bulk.

But we got continued requests to manufacture and sell Melt and Pour Soap base. My solution is this book. I decided to share these basic recipes with you to give you the freedom to make your own Melt and Pour base in the quantities that work best for your business. These recipes will teach you the foundational information that you need and give you tips on how to customize your base.

These recipes are not natural, but in reality, neither are any of the Melt and Pour Soap bases on the market today. My entire research focus has been natural cosmetics. Some may wonder why I would produce a book with recipes that aren't natural. The simple truth is, over the years I've learned there are some products that are best left to naturally-derived chemical ingredients. These would include but are not limited to Melt and Pour Soap base, hair conditioner, shampoo and hair styling products.

It is possible to make a beautiful clear natural soap with a wonderful ingredient list, but it won't re-melt for you to pour it again. In this book I give you a recipe and my soap notes to make a natural, clear soap with a similar ingredient list to what is on the market today as "Natural" Melt and Pour Soap base. This recipe is only included for those who love to experiment. It is meant to be a jumping off point for those who want to formulate a "natural" or mostly natural melt and pour soap base.

The debate over natural versus chemical cosmetics has grown over the years. My two cents is this: when it comes to wash off products like hair conditioners and styling products, I have a different philosophy than I do for products that are designed to stay on the skin. If the purpose of the product is to stay on the skin, I believe it should be as natural as possible and avoid as many chemicals as it can. A leave on product should work synergistically with your skin, and natural ingredients accomplish that better than chemical ingredients.

On the other hand, wash off products are generally cleansing agents designed to collect dirt, oil and debris and remove it all, along with the cleansing agents themselves, from your body. There are two types of cleansing agents; detergents and emulsion cleansers. I will clearly define both later in the book, but for now know that Melt and Pour Soap falls into the detergent category and true soap falls into the emulsion category. Both kinds of cleansing agents essentially have the job of removing fats and lipids, dirt, makeup and other debris from the surface of the skin. The detergent cleansing agents use a combination of surfactants to do their job.

I'm also completely comfortable with chemicals when it comes to hair conditioners. I tried a thousand and one ways to make a natural conditioner and found a thousand and one ways to make my thin, fine blonde hair look stringy, greasy and unkempt with those recipes. Then I did my research on hair conditioner and found they function in a completely different manner than the oil based natural conditioners I was creating.

Conditioner works when the pH of conditioner compacts the cuticle layer of the hair. This results in shiny, bouncy hair that is not weighed down. One of the reasons people complain about the way their hair feels when they use castile soap as a shampoo, is the pH is too high for proper hair care. The alkaline solution of castile soap makes the cuticle cells swell up and get rougher. Hair conditioner lowers the pH of your hair even further than your traditional shampoo to leave your hair fresh, easy to comb and increases the elasticity of the hair.

The conditioning ingredients in conditioners leave the hair feeling smooth, while leaving a "waxy" coating on the hair. Conditioners help with detangling because hair tangles when the cuticle layer of one hair catches on the cuticle layer of another. The conditioning ingredients form a protective coating over the cortex where the cuticle cells have broken away. The protective coating created with conditioner also seals in moisture and reduces static electricity.

All that to say, sometimes all natural or naturally derived is best and sometimes nature can benefit from a boost of chemical reactions and ingredients. Melt and Pour Soap is one of those cases.

Chapter 1

Turn Your Hobby into a Business

You might be interested in making Melt and Pour Soap from scratch as a hobby, but over the years I have seen many hobbies turn into great businesses. Since our Christmas craft project turned into a business, people often ask me when is the best time to start a new company or launch a new product line.

My answer is always the same, "Right now." It does not matter what time of the year it is, what time of your life you are in, the current state of the economy or who you are. The time that you are thinking of starting a business is the time to get started. The following 10 points are lessons learned from starting our own company and supporting thousands of start-up companies through Essential Wholesale.

1. Make a mess and clean it up later.
Don't keep getting ready to get ready; get started. If you keep sharpening your pencils and filing your files then all you will have is an organized office. Too many "would-be" entrepreneurs are stuck in the planning phase and need to just jump in. You can't grow and learn without the mistakes and lessons of actually doing the dirty work. Yes, there is a place for planning, but eventually enough is enough. Don't get stuck in the paralysis of analysis. So make a mess and clean it up later when the money starts rolling in.

2. Use your passions to pick a product line.
If you love lavender, purple or pure products, use your passion to choose your product line. But remember to keep it simple. Start with a minimum number of products. Your focus and your financial commitment should not be too broad. Don't let all your money get gobbled up getting started. You will need your capital later. Put as much focus as possible into marketing a few great products and not tons of average products. And trust your gut when you start having customers tell you that you need to add this or that product to your line. It could be simply another distraction.

3. Choose to be the Muscle or the Brain.
Some people are born marketers. Some are born to create. Others are super human and can do both. Find what you do best and do

it. Focus on your gifts and talents. If your only option is to do it all, then by all means do it all. But be smart. Decide what you want to do; make products or market them. Dennis and I changed our roles in the business depending on the season in our family's life, the stage of our business and what was needed at the time to take our business to the next level. As business owners you have to remain flexible to survive and grow.

4. Don't undersell your product.

Think ahead when setting your price point. Remember eventually you will have employees and other expenses. This is one of the most common mistakes of home businesses. Eventually you can't do it all, but you are stuck because you did not establish a large enough margin in your price point to hire help, pay yourself and grow. The choice will be either to stay small and do it all yourself, or grow and increase your price point which may result in the loss of some of your customers. It is a terrible position to be in, instead of selling your product at $3.99 to compete with Wal-Mart you should set it at $5.99 so that you have room to grow and to offer your larger customers extra pricing incentives. Business is all about thinking ahead. You can always lower your price, but it is very hard to raise it.

5. First impressions will make or break you.

Product packaging followed by product aroma is your first impression. Your product description and marketing will cause the customer to sample the goods. While you think the product itself is the most important part, in reality, to the consumer it is not as high on the list. You must have a good product to keep them coming back, but to get them to pick it up in the first place it is all about the marketing.

Invest in good packaging from your internet site design, to your brochures and (Point of Purchase) POP displays, right down to your product packaging and labels. Don't skimp on the cheapest bottle or label out there. This industry is saturated with "the best thing since sliced bread" products and the ones that get noticed are those that grab the attention of the consumer. If you need help then contact a graphic designer that has experience with personal care products. Make sure you check out their portfolio and if they don't have the type or quality of work you want for your products, then don't hire them.

6. Know your product inside and out.

You need to be able to compare and contrast your product for the average consumer and the well educated buyers alike. Translate to the consumer what makes you so passionate about your product. Keep it honest but enthusiastic. If you don't really believe in your product, no one else will either.

I am a registered and certified Aromatherapist and people insist on telling me that their product, which smells like a synthetic watermelon, is made with only pure essential oils. Since watermelons don't produce an essential oil they quickly lose their credibility with me. If you don't know what's in your product because you buy a bulk base, ask questions. They should be willing to disclose information and they must provide you with the complete ingredient list. Then learn all about those ingredients. Your customers will appreciate your knowledge and it will make the difference between you and the other guys. Do try fitting your square peg into a round hole.

7. Know who your market is.
If your price point puts you in the upper end marketplace then don't promote to the local drug store just because they saw you at a trade show and wanted your product. First they will require you to discount your product so low that it will only result in losses for you and frustration for them. Keep focused on who you are trying to reach and understand where they shop, what they buy and what motivates them to buy.

Know who your product will appeal to, often people waste time marketing to the wrong consumer for their product line. Meet the needs of your consumer group and success will follow. If you do have a "Wal-Mart" knocking on your door but you don't have a product that will meet their price point then you should consider developing a new product that can.

8. Keep your goal in front of you.
If you are creating your own business so that you can be home with your family, keep that in mind. Put photos of your kids and the vacation you want to take with them on your desk and refrigerator. Visual re-enforcement will help you through those long days and nights. And there will be days, lots of them, where you wonder why in the world you are going to all this trouble. Just remember what motivates you during those times and the little things will fade.

9. Find a mentor or someone you can count on for sound advice.
Your mentor should not be your best buddy but someone with experience in business development and more. Your local SBA

will generally have a SCORE department made up of retired business people that are looking for someone to mentor. Trust me, your family and friends just might think you are nuts starting up a company. But don't let that discourage you. Other company owners know and understand what drives you. Don't seek advice from your non-supportive best friend otherwise you could just lose your dream altogether. Your mentor needs to be someone who isn't afraid to offend you and who will point out where you are going wrong.

10. Follow the leader.
There are so many success stories in this industry and there is room for many more. A person like Donna Maria Coles Johnson of the Indie Beauty Network is just one of the exciting stories in the beauty industry. If you see the growing trend towards the mineral make-up industry, or the success of those in the five billion dollar organic products industry, follow them. Don't see competition as a negative; see it as a positive because you can always learn from them. It also means that you are positioning yourself in a hot marketplace.

Chapter 2

Basic Equipment

Investing in the right equipment for your business up front will save you time and money. In my company, Essential Wholesale, we still use many of the same stainless steel pots and utensils that we started our business with. Those pots, that are still useful today, at one time represented entire batches of products and now they are only used to warm up a small component in a batch.

Even if you are just interested in making Melt and Pour Soap from scratch as a hobby, many of the following equipment tips will still be useful in choosing the right tools you may already have in your kitchen.

Stainless Steel Cooking Pots
A good 2 to 3 gallon (8-14 quarts) stainless steel pot to cook your soap in will be worth every penny you invest. You can find great deals on stainless steel pots and equipment at used restaurant equipment and supply stores. I prefer stainless steel pots over enamel pots. Stainless steel is the easiest material to clean and sanitize prior to use. Lye will corrode most pots.

Stainless Steel Large Spoons
You will need a good stainless steel spoon for measuring, scraping, stirring and any manual mixing needed to gently release air bubbles.

Accurate Scale
A good scale can save you a lot of heartache in any manufacturing endeavor. Your ingredients should be measured out accurately for every batch. A digital scale is worth the investment. A great scale can measure from 0.002 lbs (0.032 ounce) all the way up to 20 lbs. However, a great scale can be very expensive. Look around for used and reconditioned scales. Another good option is to have two less expensive scales; one that measures all your low weights and a second that can measure higher weights.

Thermometer
You will need a thermometer that can measure up to at least 165 °F or above. My preference is a laser thermometer, but a candy or deep-fry thermometer with a stainless steel tip will work, too.

Immersion Stick Blender

You will need a good immersion stick blender, or a collection of cheap ones. This process tends to burn out immersion stick blenders so it is worth keeping an eye out for specials, coupons and deals so you can stock up on them. An immersion stick blender, also known as a hand-blender or stick blender, can be found in the kitchen department of any store.

For bigger batches, a wonderful option is to invest in a stainless steel mixer that can be attached to an electronic drill. The motor on the drill will survive longer than an immersion stick blender. An example is a Jiffy Mixer made with rust resistant stainless steel.

Goggles, Gloves, Mask and Apron

When working with and handling Sodium Hydroxide (lye) you should take extra care to protect your hands, eyes and body. Look for gloves that are chemical resistant to use while handling Sodium Hydroxide. You should also wear a mask during the initial reaction of adding the Sodium Hydroxide to water and again while adding the lye mixture to oils. A hair net should be worn during the manufacturing of all cosmetics to comply with Good Manufacturing Practices (GMP). You should also have vinegar on hand when you are working with lye as it will neutralize it should you get any on your skin.

Soap Molds

If you are going to make large batches of Melt and Pour Soap to reheat later, you may want to use slab, tray or loaf molds. For making Melt and Pour finished products you have a wide variety of soap molds to pick from including: flexible silicone molds, heavy duty molds, industrial molds and single cavity and trays molds. There are also many items around your house that can be used as soap molds. Any plastic mold will work as long as the sides are flexible and it can withstand warm liquid.

Spray Bottle with Alcohol

During the manufacturing of Melt and Pour Soap base from scratch, you will need a spray bottle of denatured alcohol or rubbing alcohol to reduce bubbles. It will also come in handy when you pour the soap in the molds to disperse the small bubbles that occur when pouring.

Chapter 3

Overview of Ingredients

Bio-Terge 804 has the INCI name: Sodium C14-16 Olefin Sulfonate, Sodium Laureth Sulfate, and Lauramide DEA. All of the ingredient information on the components of the Bio-Terge 804 can be found in this chapter under their individual INCI names.

You will find that in the ingredient lists provided with the recipes the individual components fall lower than you might expect. This is because the breakdown of the separate components makes each separate INCI name fall lower in the ingredient deck.

Castor Oil, USP is a thick, viscous vegetable oil extracted from the seed of the castor plant. It is used commercially in 50% of lipsticks in the United States. Castor Oil creates a soothing, protective barrier on the skin. It also acts as a humectant by drawing moisture from the air and holding it to the skin.

Castor Oil is a triglyceride that is mainly composed of ricinoleic acid (87%), which gives castor oil solvent-like properties useful in manufacturing a transparent soap. Ricinoleic acid is a monounsaturated, 18-carbon fatty acid that has an unusual hydroxyl functional group on the twelfth carbon. It is this functional group that makes castor oil unusually polar.

Cocoamidopropyl Betaine, MPS is a fairly mild and gentle surfactant used in melt and pour soaps, shampoos, conditioners, and body washes. It has been valued for its foaming qualities and, ability to serve as a thickening agent. Cocoamidopropyl betaine leaves hair and skin soft and smooth. It is compatible with other cationic, anionic, and nonionic surfactants making it a favorite of cosmetic formulators. Cocamidopropyl betaine has an exceptional safety profile and performs markedly well.

Cocamidopropyl betaine is a long chain surfactant derived from coconut oil. Skeptics are alarmed by the fact that during the synthesis of this ingredient, some of the reagents involved in the reaction may be potentially harmful. A solid comprehension of the chemistry involved in reagents will help clarify this debate. A reagent is a substance that is used in a chemical reaction to produce other substances. It is not in the final product. An example of this could be the Sodium Hydroxide when it is used to cause a reaction called saponification to create soap. Sodium Hydroxide is an ingredient with multiple hazard warnings, but when combined with other constituents it creates an effective, safe, and diverse cleaning agent. There is no un-reacted Sodium Hydroxide in the finished soap because a new product has been formed. In addition, the Cocamidopropyl betaine MPS called for in the recipes in this book has 0 ppm (parts per million) amidoamines and absolutely no un-reacted reagents left in it.

The Cosmetic Ingredient Review (CIR) Expert Panel reviewed Cocamidopropyl betaine and found it to be safe for use as used in rinse of products and limited it to 3% for leave-on products. According to the general provisions of the Cosmetics Directive of the European Union, Cocamidopropyl betaine may be used in cosmetics and personal care products marketed in Europe. In tests Cocoamidopropyl betaine was found to be readily biodegradable, slightly orally toxic, moderately irritating to the eyes, mildly irritating to the skin, and no delayed contact hypersensitivity or evidence of sensitization was observed. It is not a mutagenic, nor is it a carcinogen. Cocamidopropyl betaine is an excellent example of how information has been misused by organizations with an agenda. For example, according to Skin Deep, Cocamidopropyl betaine is rated as a moderate hazard due to: "Violations, Restrictions & Warning, Allergies/immunotoxicity, Contamination Concerns, and Ecotoxicology."

After thorough research over the rating of Cocamidopropyl betaine, I found not only was the rating system fatally flawed, but it is used to misrepresent the truth. I have added the Addendum I , Skin Deep and Cocomidopropyl Betaine Debate in this book to review the topic of misinformation to help consumers decipher the ratings given to Cocamidopropyl betaine by Skin Deep.

Disclaimer: *There are several different trade names for Cocamidopropyl betaine with minor variations of solids, color, pH, cloud point and viscosity. All of the formulas in this book were done using Cocamidopropyl betaine, MPS. Results may vary with another version of Cocamidopropyl betaine.*

Coconut Oil has a small molecular structure which allows it to be easily absorbed by the skin. It leaves the skin feeling soft and smooth but not oily. Coconut oil is great for the skin because of its antioxidant properties, which also contributes to its long shelf life. The antioxidants in coconut oil stop the chain reaction of free-radicals creating more free-radicals. Because of the antioxidants, coconut oil not only softens your skin but protects it from further damage, while promoting healthy skin. Coconut oil is also the richest source of good medium chain fatty acids, which our sebum also produces as a protective layer on the skin to kill harmful germs.

Coconut oil is a vegetable sourced oil that is naturally free of the need for pesticides and other chemicals to grow and harvest. Some of the myths about coconut oil come from the belief in post World War II times that coconut contained high levels of cholesterol, which internally or topically would result in acne. Current research on the chemical composition of coconut oil has proven that it does not contain cholesterol at all. Coconut oil contains lauric acid, which actually supports the antibacterial activity of the skin's cells.

Coconut oil is the number one oil used to make surfactants and soap because it produces a nice lather. Some surfactant based cleansers for oily skin are formulated to strip the skin, and they do leave it feeling dry, and coconut is incorrectly blamed. Typically, cleansers that are formulated for oily skin are designed to strip away the oily layer on the skin. Many consumers feel that their skin is truly clean in this state. However, the skin produces more oil when it is stripped because it becomes dry and, a vicious cycle of oily, dry, oily, dry skin is created.

Coconut oil contains the fatty acids caprylic acid, capric acid and lauric acid. Many of the coconut derived ingredients can be identified easily by these fatty acids. Coconut oil consists of 90% saturated fat. It is made mostly of medium chain triglycerides which are 92% saturated fatty acids (44.6% lauric acid, 16.8% myristic acid, 8.2% palmitic acid, 8% caprylic acid), 6% monounsaturated fatty acids (oleic acid) and 2% polyunsaturated fatty acids (linoleic acid). The lauric acid in coconut oil helps create a hard soap bar that is cleansing with a light fluffy lather. Coconut melts at 76°F but if stored at a cooler temperature it is solid. Coconut oil resists rancidity because it is slow to oxidize.

Denatured Alcohol, or Ethanol, is used in making transparent soap. When you buy denatured alcohol to make soap you should search for one that is labeled SDA 3A or SDA 3C. These Specially Denatured Alcohols (SDA) are approved for use in cosmetics by the U.S. Food and Drug Administration (FDA). When alcohol is being used for anything other than food, beverages or oral drugs the government requires that it be denatured. In order to do that, a small amount of a denaturant is added to grain alcohol in order to make it taste unappealing.

The other option, and often more expensive one, is to buy 190 proof ClearSprings or Everclear at your local liquor store. Whichever one you chose will work fine, but don't try to substitute either with rubbing alcohol (isopropyl alcohol).

Glycerin, also referred to as Glycerol, is a sugar alcohol that is obtained by adding alkalies to fats and fixed oils. Glycerin is a soothing humectant that draws moisture from the air to the skin. It is an emollient, which makes the skin feel softer and smoother. Glycerin has a high hydrophilic (water) factor and a low lipophilic (fat) factor. It is completely miscible with water.

The FDA includes Glycerin on its list of direct food additives considered Generally Recognized As Safe (GRAS), and on its list of approved indirect food additives. Glycerin is also an FDA approved active ingredient in Over-the-Counter (OTC) skin protectant drug products, ear drying products and it's an approved demulcent for the eyes.

While Glycerin has been added to the Canadian Hotlist, there is no need to panic. Health Canada simply wants a copy of a DEG Free certificate to ensure glycerin used in cosmetics is not contaminated with diethylene glycol (DEG).

The FDA and the U.S. Pharmacopia recently adopted new standards for glycerin. The requirement of a DEG certificate is due to Chinese glycerin, used in oral medications, which had been adulterated with ethylene glycol and diethylene glycol. The practice of switching ethylene glycol as a cheap substitute for glycerin goes back as far as 1937 when more than 107 people were killed in the United States by ethylene glycol used as a liquid base for antibiotics. In recent history, there have been cases of ethylene glycol or diethylene glycol contamination found in toothpaste from China in the United States and Panama. The latest case of DEG tainted glycerin occurred in November, 2008 when 84 Nigerian children died after being given a tainted teething drug.

The FDA issued a warning after it received reports about fatal DEG poisoning of consumers who ingested medicinal syrups, such as cough syrup or acetaminophen syrup, that were manufactured with DEG-contaminated glycerin from China. This caused the FDA to set up Guidance for Industry testing of glycerin for diethylene glycol through the Center for Drug Evaluation and Research (CDER). The FDA asked the USP to improve the standard for glycerin to exclude ehtylene glycol and diethylene glycol from glycerin. The new standards were set up to ensure tainted drugs are no longer being sold. It also provides a DEG Free certificate for the cosmetic industry that can be used to document our cosmetics are diethylene glycol free.

According to the general provisions of the Cosmetics Directive of the European Union, Glycerin may be used in cosmetics and personal care products marketed in Europe. Glycerin derived from raw materials of animal origin must comply with European Union animal by-products regulations. The Joint FAO/WHO Expert Committee on Food Additives has not specified an acceptable daily intake for Glycerin. Glycerol is considered to be readily biodegradable in the aquatic environment.

Lauramide DEA is a fatty acid derivative of diethanolamine (DEA*). It is a nonionic surfactant used in the formulation of shampoos, hair dyes, bath products and lotions as a viscosity booster and, to increase and stabilize the foaming capacity of a formula. Lauramide DEA also thickens the aqueous portion of a formula. Lauramide DEA is produced from naturally occurring lauric acid.

The CIR Expert Panel concluded that Lauramide DEA was safe as a cosmetic ingredient. The CIR Expert Panel reviewed data on Lauramide DEA showing that: it is slightly toxic to nontoxic via acute oral administration; it is not a dermal toxin in acute and sub-chronic studies; it is a mild skin irritant but not a sensitizer or photosensitizer; it is a mild to moderate eye irritant; it does not demonstrate mutagenic activity.

Lauramide DEA is listed under Fatty Acid Dialkylamides and Dialkanolamides in the Cosmetics Directive of the European Union (see Annex III, Part I) and may be used with a maximum secondary amine concentration of 0.5%. It may not be used with nitrosating systems. In the Cosmetics Directive of the European Union, Lauramide DEA was lumped into the Fatty Acid Dialkylamides and Dialkanolamides along with Cocamide DEA, Linoleamide DEA and Oleamide DEA. The CIR Expert Panel determined that only Cocamide DEA should not be used with nitrosating systems.

*Since Lauramide DEA is a fatty acid derivative of diethanolamine (DEA) I wanted to take a moment to address the safety data regarding DEA. DEA has been assessed by the CIR Expert Panel and concluded they that DEA is safe for use in cosmetics and personal care products designed for discontinuous, brief use followed by thorough rinsing from the surface of the skin. In products intended for prolonged contact with the skin, the concentration of DEA should not exceed 5%.

Myristic Acid is a digestible non-toxic fatty acid that occurs naturally in some foods, such as animal fats and most vegetables. Nutmeg, palm oil and coconut oil contain relatively high levels of Myristic Acid. The saturated fatty acid Myristic Acid has 14 carbon atoms. Myristic Acid is used as a cleansing, surfactant and opacifying agent in cosmetics and personal care products.

The safety of Myristic Acid has been assessed by the CIR Expert Panel and they concluded that Myristic Acid is safe as a cosmetic ingredient in the present practices of use and concentration. The CIR Expert Panel recognizes that the salts of Myristic Acid dissociate to form Myristic Acid and esters of Myristic Acid are hydrolyzed to their corresponding alcohols and Myristic Acid which are then further metabolized. Myristic Acid is not a dermal irritant and is minimally irritating to the eyes.

According to the general provisions of the Cosmetics Directive of the European Union, Myristic Acid may be used in cosmetics and personal care products in Europe. If it is derived from animal sources, it must comply with the European Union animal by-products regulations.

You will notice that the recipes call for Myristic Acid but the ingredient lists list it as Sodium Myristate. This is because the Sodium Hydroxide saponifies the Myristic Acid and creates a new ingredient called Sodium Myristate.

Palm Oil is derived from the fruits of palm trees. It is used in soapmaking to create a hard long-lasting soap bar with a creamy stable lather. Palm oil is a valuable source of vitamin E (360-600 ppm) and a variety of carotenoids (vitamin A). Palm oil has a natural fatty acid profile that makes it valuable in the cosmetic, soap and food industries. Palm oil is excellent for use in clear soaps and it saponifies quickly. The fatty acid composition of palm oil is myristic acid (1.1%), palmitic acid (44%), stearic acid (4.5%), oleic acid (39.2%), linoleic acid (10.1%), lauric acid (0.02%) and others (0.9%).

Propylene glycol is a colorless, odorless liquid that is miscible with water. Propylene glycol is one of the most widely used ingredients in cosmetics. It is also used in foods and pharmaceuticals. Propylene Glycol is a skin conditioning agent that has the ability to attract water and act as a moisturizer in cosmetic formulas.

Propylene glycol is GRAS by the FDA. The safety of Propylene Glycol has been assessed by the CIR Expert Panel and they concluded that Propylene Glycol is safe for use in cosmetic products at concentrations up to 50%. The concentration limit of Propylene Glycol that was set by the CIR Expert Panel was based on the results of human irritation and sensitization tests, because it was noted that patients with diseased skin may be susceptible to developing irritation/sensitization reactions to Propylene Glycol.

The National Toxicology Program's (NTP) Center for the Evaluation of Risk to Human Reproduction (CERHR) Expert Panel in 2003 reviewed the reproductive and developmental effect of Propylene Glycol. The CERHR Expert Panel concluded there is "negligible concern for reproductive or developmental toxicity to humans." Propylene glycol is listed in the United States Pharmacopoeia and is included in New and Non-Official Remedies as a proper ingredient for pharmaceutical products.

According to the general provisions of the Cosmetics Directive of the European Union, Propylene Glycol may be used in cosmetics and personal care products marketed in Europe. The Joint FAO/WHO Expert Committee on Food Additives recommends a maximum daily oral intake of 25 mg Propylene Glycol/kg body weight/day.

Propylene glycol is not acutely toxic, it is essentially non-irritating to the skin, not a sensitizer and mildly irritating to the eyes. Studies of Propylene glycol have shown that it does not cause reproductive, developmental, teratogenic, genotoxic effect and it is not a carcinogen. It is readily biodegraded in water or soil.

Many of the misconceptions about Propylene Glycol are based on inaccurate information caused by confusing it with another ingredient, Ethylene Glycol. Ethylene Glycol is toxic and is widely used as automobile antifreeze; Propylene Glycol is not.

Sodium Hydroxide (NaOH) is a water soluble white which occur in flakes, pellets, granules and powders. Sodium Hydroxide is commonly used in the formulation of bath products, cleansing products, shampoos and shaving products. Sodium Hydroxide is also used to hydrolyze fats (as in saponification) and form soaps. It is also known as caustic soda and soda lye.

Sodium Hydroxide is created via electrolysis of sodium chloride. Sodium Hydroxide is a strong alkaline substance that dissociates completely in water to sodium and hydroxyl ions. This creates a strong exothermic reaction when it is added to water. Sodium Hydroxide is an inorganic base, which means it is an alkali containing no carbon atoms. Sodium Hydroxide separates into cations (positively charged sodium) and hydroxide anions (negatively charged) when added to water and the hydroxide anions decrease the acidity of the water (increasing the pH). This is why Sodium Hydroxide is commonly used as a pH adjuster in formulas.

Concentrated Sodium Hydroxide is a strong irritant and corrosive to the skin, eyes, respiratory tract and gastrointestinal system if ingested. The severity of effects caused by Sodium Hydroxide is a function of the concentration, the pH, the length of tissue contact time and local conditions and skin type. Protective equipment such as rubber gloves, safety clothing, face mask and eye protection should always be used when handling Sodium Hydroxide or its solutions. Proper ventilation should always be used when handling or reacting Sodium Hydroxide. Sodium Hydroxide should be stored in airtight containers because it readily absorbs the water in the air.

The FDA includes Sodium Hydroxide on its list of substances affirmed as GRAS for direct addition to food. The Joint FAO/WHO Expert Committee on Food Additives has not limited the Acceptable Daily Intake of Sodium Hydroxide. Sodium Hydroxide is listed in the Cosmetics Directive of the European Union (see Annex III), and may be used at the specific concentrations, pH values and warning labels when it is used in nail cuticle solvents, hair straighteners and in depilatories. It can be up to pH 11 for other uses as a pH adjuster.

You should always have a current Material Safety Data Sheet (MSDS) on hand when using Sodium Hydroxide.

You will notice that the recipes call for Sodium Hydroxide but the ingredient list does not include it. This is because the Sodium Hydroxide saponifies the Stearic Acid and Myristic and creates new ingredients called Sodium Stearate and Sodium Myristate. In other words, what goes into the pot are Sodium Hydroxide, Stearic Acid and Myristic Acid, but what comes out of the pot are Sodium Stearate and Sodium Myristate.

Sodium C14-16 Olefin Sulfonate (a Sodium Alpha-Olefin Sulfonate) is a mixture of long chain sulfonate salts prepared by the sulfonation of alpha olefins. The numbers (14-16) indicate the average lengths of the carbon chains of the alpha olefins. It is most commonly used in shampoos and bath and shower products. Sodium C14-16 Olefin Sulfonate helps clean the skin and hair by helping the water from your shower or bath to mix with the oil and dirt on your body and hair so they can be rinsed away.

The FDA reviewed the safety of Sodium C14-16 Olefin Sulfonate as indirect food additives, as components of adhesives, and as emulsifiers and/or surface-active agents. The safety of Sodium C14-16 Olefin Sulfonate has been assessed by the CIR Expert Panel and they concluded that it was safe as used in rinse-off products and safe up to 2% in leave-on products.

The CIR Expert Panel noted that Sodium Alpha-Olefin Sulfonates are poorly absorbed through normal skin but significantly absorbed through damaged skin. Short-term toxicity studies showed no consistent effects. High concentrations produced moderate to mild ocular irritation. At doses that were maternally toxic they found fetal abnormalities in animal studies. Genotoxicity, oral and dermal studies were negative.

Some studies found irritation and sensitization. This sensitization was attributed to low level gamma sultone residues. Because gamma sultones were sensitizers at very low levels, it was concluded that any product containing Sodium Alpha-Olefin Sulfonates should have very little gamma sultone residues. The gamma sultone levels should not exceed 10 ppm for saturated (alkane) sultones, 1 ppm for chlorosultones, and 0.1 ppm for unsaturated sultones. Sodium Alpha-Olefin Sulfonates are otherwise considered safe for use in rinse-off products. The use of Sodium Alpha-Olefin Sulfonates in leave-on products is limited to 2% in a formula.

According to the general provisions of the Cosmetics Directive of the European Union, Sodium C14-16 Olefin Sulfonate may be used in cosmetics and personal care products marketed in Europe.

Sodium Laureth Sulfate (SLES) is a very effective cleansing agent that belongs to the chemical class of alkyl ether sulfates. It is a salt of sulfated ethoxylated fatty alcohol and is the most commonly used of the alkyl ether sulfates that are used in cleansing products, including bubble baths, bath soaps and detergents and shampoos.

SLES exhibits emulsifying properties and imparts "softness" to the skin. As a cleansing agent the anionic surfactant SLES wets body surfaces, emulsifies or solubilize oils and suspends soil. It also contributes to the lathering properties and excellent viscosity response in cleansing products and bubble baths formulas. Sodium Laureth Sulfate exhibits a high degree of foaming. SLES was formulated to improved mildness over Sodium Lauryl Sulfate (SLS).

The safety of SLES was assessed in 1983 and re-reviewed in 2002 by the CIR Expert Panel and they concluded SLES is safe for use in cosmetics and personal care products in the present practices of use and concentration when formulated to be non-irritating. It can cause mild to moderate skin irritation in some people. According to the general provisions of the Cosmetics Directive of the European Union, Sodium Laureth Sulfate may be used in cosmetics and personal care products that are marketed in Europe.

SLES did not result in adverse effects in numerous safety studies including acute, sub-chronic and chronic oral exposure, reproductive and developmental toxicity, carcinogenic, photosensitization studies and SLES readily biodegrades.

Despite internet rumors SLES is not a carcinogenic substance. The World Health Organization, the International Agency for the Research of Cancer, US Environment Protection Agency and the European Union are all organizations that classify and register all substances that are known to be carcinogenic. None of these organizations have classified SLES as a carcinogen.

Sorbitol, also known as sugar alcohol, is a naturally occurring polyalcohol. It is prepared for commercial use by the hydrogenation of glucose. It is also found naturally in berries, cherries, plums, pears, seaweed, apples and algae. It is commonly used as a sugar substitute in foods, especially for diabetics. In cosmetics it is commonly used in aftershave lotions, mild soaps and baby shampoos. Sorbitol is used as a humectant and skin conditioning agent. The FDA includes Sorbitol on the list of direct food substances affirmed as GRAS. The safety of Sorbitol was also assessed by the Joint FAO/WHO Expert Committee on Food Additives, and it was concluded that it is not necessary to limit the dietary intake of Sorbitol. According to the general provisions of the Cosmetics Directive of the European Union, Sorbitol may be used in cosmetics and personal care products marketed in Europe.

Stearic Acid is a waxy fatty acid that naturally occurs in some foods including vegetable fats and oils and animals. It is commonly used in a variety of cosmetic creams, lotions and soaps as a surfactant, cleansing agent and emulsifying agent. It can be derived from either animal tallow or from a vegetable source.

The FDA includes Stearic Acid on its list of direct food additives considered GRAS and it is permitted as a direct food additive in chewing gum base and foods. The safety of Stearic Acid has been assessed by the CIR Expert Panel and they concluded these ingredients were safe for use in cosmetic products. The CIR Expert Panel noted that Stearic Acid is a fatty acid with a hydrocarbon chain of 18 carbons with a terminal carboxyl group.

In chronic studies of Stearic Acid there were no adverse effects observed at high doses and few effects were observed in acute toxicity tests. Topical application of Stearic Acid to the skin produced little or no apparent toxicity. Stearic Acid is not a sensitizer or photosensitizing agent, not an eye or skin irritant, and not carcinogenic.

According to the general provisions of the Cosmetics Directive of the European Union, Stearic Acid may be used in cosmetics and personal care products marketed in Europe. If it is derived from animal sources, it must comply with European Union animal by-products regulations.

You will notice that the recipes call for Stearic Acid but the ingredient lists list it as Sodium Stearate. This is because the Sodium Hydroxide saponifies the Stearic Acid and creates a new ingredient called Sodium Stearate.

Titanium Dioxide is a naturally occurring mineral derived from oxide of titanium. It is used to impart whiteness to color cosmetics and personal care products that are applied to the skin, to increase the opacity, and reduce the transparency of a finished product. Titanium Dioxide is used in White Melt and Pour Soap to create the white color. You will also find it in other Melt and Pour Soaps on the market to impart a white color, such as Shea Butter and Goat's Milk bases.

Titanium Dioxide is an important ingredient used in sunscreen products. Sunscreens are regulated by the FDA as Over-The-Counter (OTC) drug products. But this doesn't mean you should say your soap acts as a sunscreen! First of all, it doesn't since it is a wash off product. And secondly, making a sunscreen claim would put your soap under OTC drug regulations.
The FDA has assessed the safety of Titanium Dioxide as a color additive for use in food, drugs and cosmetics. The FDA set regulations approving the Titanium Dioxide for each of these purposes. As a cosmetic, the FDA has stated, "The color additive titanium dioxide may be safely used in cosmetics, including

cosmetics intended for use in the area of the eye, in amounts consistent with good manufacturing practice."

According to the Cosmetics Directive of the European Union, Titanium Dioxide is listed as Colour Index (CI) No. 77891 in the Cosmetics Directive of the European Union as an allowed color additive (Annex IV, Part I), and may be used without restriction according to the purity requirements that have been established for the quality of the same material used in foods. Europe also allows Titanium Dioxide to be used as a sunscreen active ingredient to protect against the adverse effects of ultraviolet radiation found in sunlight.

Triethanolamine (TEA) is a clear, viscous liquid used to reduce the surface tension in emulsions. This allows the water-soluble and oil-soluble ingredients in a formula to blend better. It is a strong base, which makes it useful in adjusting the pH of a cosmetic formula. TEA is completely soluble in water and is rapidly biodegradable.

TEA neutralizes fatty acids and solubilizes oils and other ingredients that are not completely soluble in water. TEA combines the properties of both amines and alcohols and can undergo reactions common to both groups. As an amine, TEA reacts with acids because it is mildly alkaline, and forms soaps. When TEA acts as an alcohol it is hygroscopic and can cause the esterification of free fatty acids. You will see in our recipes the addition of TEA to a recipe will create crystal clear soap.

TEA can solidify or crystallize in cool temperatures because the freezing point is 70.9 °F. If your TEA is not a viscous pourable liquid when you receive it, simply give the container a warm water bath.

The FDA includes TEA on its list of indirect food additives, which means TEA may be used in adhesives in contact with food and to assist in the washing or peeling of fruits and vegetables. The safety of TEA has been assessed by the CIR Expert Panel and they concluded that TEA is safe for use in cosmetics and personal care products designed for discontinuous, brief use followed by thorough rinsing from the surface of the skin. In products intended for prolonged contact with the skin, the concentration of TEA should not exceed 5%.

TEA is lumped in with some other ingredients that have earned it the warning, "should not be used in products containing N-nitrosating agents to prevent the formation of nitrosamines." However, because TEA is a tertiary amine, it does not react with nitrosating agents to produce nitrosamines. Using very sensitive analytical tools, a study by the Regulatory Toxicology and Pharmacology found when TEA was ingested with sodium nitrite, no significant nitrosamine formation was found. The CIR Expert Panel also recognized that TEA is a mild skin and eye irritants and irritation increased with elevated concentrations, which again is why formulations should not exceed 5%. TEA is a good example of how animal testing, where animals are given large doses of an ingredient, does not translate accurately to human topical application. In one study by the National Toxicology Program, there was in increased occurrence of liver tumors in mice that were dosed dermally with TEA over their lifetime. However, in another study it did not cause tumors in rats treated the same or in mice that were genetically engineered to be more sensitive. It also did not damage genetic material. Research has now proven the most likely cause of tumors in the mice that formed liver tumors was due to the TEA causing a deficiency in choline. Humans are resistant to the development of choline deficiency and test animals are not. In addition, cosmetics that use TEA are not ingested, nor is it applied dermally at 100% concentrations over your lifetime.

Chapter 4

Material Data Safety Sheet and You

A very common question many in the cosmetic and soap industry is: should I collect a Material Safety Data Sheet (MSDS) or not? The best way to answer that question is with a thorough understanding of what a MSDS is designed to do.

The MSDS is a single document prepared by the manufacturer that contains all the information about the chemical make-up, use, storage, handling, emergency procedures and the potential health effects related to a hazardous material. MSDS was originally intended for hazardous materials only in order to comply with Federal regulations. However, now many materials with no hazards have an MSDS simply for product liability purposes alone.

Today an ingredient that has an MSDS is not necessarily a hazardous material or causes health effects. Much of the information from the MSDS information is misused to make an ingredient look bad in personal care items, as is the practice of organizations like the Environmental Working Group and their database Skin Deep. The fact is that an MSDS sheet is simply giving information about the safe handling of the ingredient at full concentration, which does not translate to normal cosmetic usage, since you never use any ingredient at 100% concentration in any cosmetic formula.

A perfect example of how the MSDS does not translate to the finished product is with lye. The MSDS shows that it causes eye, skin, digestive and respiratory burns. However, in the finished product it causes no ill effect to the consumer. Unfortunately, those with regulatory agendas misuse the MSDS information to create propaganda against many ingredients that are perfectly safe in the finished product.

All MSDS information is required to contain the same uniform categories of information including: chemical identity, health hazard data, manufacturer information, precautions for safe handling and use, hazardous ingredients, exposure controls/personal protection, physical/chemical properties as well as fire and explosion hazard data. The purpose of an MSDS is to inform you of proper handling of a material, first aid treatment, accident response protocol, effect on human health, chemicals with which it can adversely react, as well as the chemical make-up and physical properties prior to usage. When new regulatory information or health effects information becomes available the MSDS must be updated.

Many are concerned that the MSDS is hard to interpret. That is because the original purpose of an MSDS was for industrial hygienists, chemical engineers and safety professionals who were trained to read them. The MSDS has become more widely used but the language was never changed to laymen terms. The MSDS is often used by employers, employees, emergency responders, freight forwarders, soap makers and home crafters. Sometimes you may find an MSDS formatted differently by some manufacturers, but they all contain the exact same information required by law. Once you get the hang of reading MSDS you won't even notice the differences.

If you are manufacturing with raw materials you should get a copy of the MSDS for your knowledge and records. The most important parts to read include the name of the material, hazards, safe handling, storage requirements, and emergency procedures. Store the MSDS in a file that will be easy to access if emergency responders such as Occupational Safety & Health Administration (OSHA), fire fighters, hazardous material crews, emergency medical technicians and emergency room personnel need them.

If you have employees, you are required by law to maintain readily accessible MSDS for any "known to be present" hazardous materials in the workplace. The MSDS is designed for employees who will occupationally come in contact with hazardous materials. OSHA Hazard Communication Standard requires that safety training on proper handling of materials be conducted and all hazardous materials be labeled appropriately. If you have contractors on the premises you must inform them of the potential hazards. The MSDS is designed to help employers and employees protect themselves from hazardous chemical exposures and to teach them to handle material safely. Not only is it important to take all those steps but it is critical to log and document it all.

Are you left wondering if you need to collect MSDS sheets or not? The answer is simple. Do any of the ingredients you use have a hazardous rating above zero? Do you use lye? Do you have employees? If the answer to any one of these questions is yes, you must collect MSDS for ingredients you use with a hazard rating above zero.

The National Fire Protection Association (NFPA) believes that the MSDS and labeling of material with the NFPA hazard diamond are relevant for anything flammable. The NFPA hazard diamond uses a standard system for identification of hazardous of materials for emergency response. You don't really want your emergency responder to have to read the whole sheet. Instead, the NFPA hazard diamond on the material will tell them everything they need to know in a glance.

Chapter 5

Lye Handling Safety Tips

Warning, warning, warning! I cannot stress enough the importance of handling the Sodium Hydroxide and the resulting lye solution with caution. Sodium Hydroxide, in or out of solution, is quite caustic and can cause chemical burns on contact.

The amount of lye used in manufacturing Melt and Pour Soap is much smaller than traditional soap. However it should still be treated with great respect and caution.

- Always store sodium hydroxide in a well-sealed, appropriately marked and break-proof container out of the reach of children and pets.

- Always wear safety goggles, chemical resistant gloves, a mask and appropriate skin coverings when handling Sodium Hydroxide raw flakes or the resulting lye solution.

- Always use the appropriate vessel to create your lye solution. Always use a heavy glass container, Pyrex, stainless steel or heavy plastic container. I prefer stainless steel or a large heavy Pyrex measuring cup. Having a pour spout on the lye vessel will make adding the lye solution to your formula safer.

- Always add the water to the vessel first and then slowly add the Sodium Hydroxide. Stir thoroughly with a stainless steel spoon. Warning: If you add water to Sodium Hydroxide you will get a dangerous volcano. One of our customer service reps, Kathy, is an avid soapmaker and she taught me the jiggle, "it (lye) always snows on water" as a reminder that lye should always be added on top of water and not vice versa.

- Always use room temperature water to create your lye solution. You do not need to heat up the water first because Sodium Hydroxide creates an exothermic reaction that will automatically raise the temperature of your lye solution.

- When handling lye always be sure that your time will be uninterrupted and free of children and pets. Keep your focus on safely handling lye during the time you are working with it.

- Work in a well ventilated area when mixing sodium hydroxide. The reaction gives off a small vapor that is slightly toxic. Using the hood vent in your kitchen is a good extra measure of caution.

- You must have the MSDS for Sodium Hydroxide on hand if you manufacture with it.

- Keep Sodium Hydroxide in its original packaging. It should be clearly labeled as Sodium Hydroxide. It should have the NFPA 704 Diamond Placard for lye (Sodium Hydroxide) with a red, yellow, white and blue image. The label must have the appropriate warnings such as: DANGER, CAUTION or WARNING, "Harmful if Swallowed", "Causes Burns", Danger or Poison, Keep out of Reach of Children.

- **First Aid:** Danger-Poison! Corrosive: Causes eye damage and severe skin burns!

- **If swallowed:** Rinse mouth with water and drink one or two glasses of water. Do not induce vomiting! Immediately get medical attention or call your poison control center at **1-800-222-1222**.

- **If in eyes:** Immediately flush eyes with water. Remove any contact lenses and continue to flush eyes with water for at least 20 minutes. Immediately get medical attention or call your poison control center at **1-800-222-1222**.

The following instructions are from the official MSDS instructions. They are contrary to what soap makers do in the case of contact with lye. However, I am including them to be thorough.

- **If on skin:** Gently wipe product from skin and remove any contaminated clothing. Flush skin with plenty of water for at least 15 minutes and then wash thoroughly with soap and water. Contact a physician or call your poison control center at **1-800-222-1222**.

However many soapers follow the first aid measures below because lye is an alkaline and vinegar is an acid, which creates a balanced pH:

- Avoid water when you get powdered lye on your skin. Your first instinct will be to wash it off with water; however with powdered lye, this will cause more burns. Instead of water, douse the area with vinegar immediately to neutralize the lye.

- If you get liquid lye on your skin, pour running water over the area and then douse the area in vinegar. The water will dilute the lye solution and then the vinegar can stop or slow the burning process.

Chapter 6

From Scratch Melt and Pour Soap Recipes

If you are like me, you might have skipped the previous chapters and jumped right into the recipes. If you did, stop here and read the chapters Basic Equipment and Lye Handling Safety Tips before you proceed with any of these recipes. Also, before you start to sell your soaps I highly recommend reading the entire book, but especially the chapter Overview of Ingredients; Is it a Soap, Cosmetic or Drug?; The INCI Language of Cosmetics Ingredient Lists; and Good Manufacturing Practices.

 ## Basic Melt & Pour Soap Base Formula
10 lbs (160 ounces)

Phase Zero: Before starting any manufacturing project, sanitize the surface area you will be working on and all equipment, pots and utensils you will use in the process. Refer to GMP section of the book for more detailed instructions.

Phase 1: Create Lye Solution by Mixing

Caution: Always wear safety gear, work in a ventilated area, use the appropriate vessel (stainless steel, Pyrex, heavy glass or plastic) and add the lye to the water and not vice versa. See Lye Safety Tips for more detailed information prior to doing Phase 1.

4.75 ounces De-ionized or Distilled Water
4.75 ounces Sodium Hydroxide

Clearly mark the lye mixture and set aside until asked for the lye solution in phase 4.

NOTE: Dissolving lye to 50% solution can sometimes be tricky. It is about the max load that the water can take. Be SURE the lye is completely dissolved; make sure it doesn't get too cool as it may start to re-crystallize at 50 °F. Lye solution will be safest to handle between 135 °F and 160 °F.

Phase 2: Measure and then Heat While Mixing
29.75 ounces Propylene Glycol

11.45 ounces Vegetable Glycerin
31.25 ounces 70% Sorbitol Solution
47.6 ounces Bio-Terge 804

Phase 3: When Temperature of Phase 2 Reaches 140 °F Add and Mix
20.8 ounces Stearic Acid
9.7 ounces Myristic Acid

Phase 4: When temperature of Phase 3 reaches 165 °F slowly add lye solution in a thin slow stream from Phase 1 and mix. Intermitted (alternately stopping and starting again every few minutes) mix for about 20 minutes or until the soap base is transparent.

Phase 5: Discontinue mixing and let batch sit on heat for 1 hour at 165 °F. If you want super clear soap skip ahead to phase 7.

Phase 6: Check for excessive fatty acids to ensure clarity of the batch. This can be done by one of the following two methods.

1. Pull a very small sample and allow it to cool completely. If when it is completely cooled (not warm at all) it is clear then your batch is ready to pour. You can speed up the cooling process by putting the sample in an artificially cooled area such as a refrigerator or freezer. If it appears cloudy then follow Phase 7.

2. Perform a cold water test similar to how you check hardness in candy. Fill a cup with cold water and drop about ½ tsp into the cold water. If the soap turns obviously cloudy follow Phase 7.

Phase 7: Add and gently stir into hot soap base (155 °F and 165 °F)
1.6 ounces Myristic Acid
4.15 ounces Triethanolamine TEA

Phase 8: For best results pour into soap molds between 150 °F and 155 °F.

Phase 9: Spray surface of soap with denatured alcohol to eliminate bubbles created while pouring warm soap into molds.

If for any reason you are not happy with the clarity of your batch you can reheat it and add 0.5% to 1% more TEA.

INCI Ingredient List if you did not add TEA
Propylene Glycol, Vegetable Glycerin, Sorbitol, Sodium Stearate, Sodium

Myristate, Sodium C14-16 Olefin Sulfonate, Sodium Laureth Sulfate, Lauramide DEA.

INCI Ingredient List if you did add TEA
Propylene Glycol, Vegetable Glycerin, Sorbitol, Sodium Stearate, Sodium Myristate, Sodium C14-16 Olefin Sulfonate, Sodium Laureth Sulfate, Lauramide DEA, Triethanolamine.

Soap Notes: Attempted to lower lye in the formula by using SAP values of Stearic Acid and Myristic Acid – batch failed. Attempted to remove Propylene Glycol from the formula – batch failed. Attempted to replace Propylene Glycol with Glycerin – batch failed. Attempted to replace Propylene Glycol with Hyaluronic Acid – batch failed. Tried different Surfactant Blends – batches failed. Added 1% and 2% additional Myristic Acid in phase 3 – both batches passed. This is the basic foundation of all the other formula so I did not repeat the above experiments on the other formulas. What for Soap Notes that explain specific experiments performed on each recipe.

Your Soap Notes:

Crystal Clear Melt & Pour Soap Base
10 lbs (160 ounces)

Phase Zero: Before starting any manufacturing project, sanitize the surface area you will be working on and all equipment, pots and utensils that you will use in the process. Refer to GMP section of the book for more detailed instructions.

Phase 1: Create Lye Solution by Mixing

Caution: Always wear safety gear, work in a ventilated area, use the appropriate vessel (stainless steel, Pyrex, heavy glass or plastic) and add the lye to the water and not vice versa. See Lye Safety Tips for more detailed information prior to doing Phase 1.

4.86 ounces De-ionized or Distilled Water
4.86 ounces Sodium Hydroxide

Clearly mark the lye mixture and set aside until asked for the lye solution in phase 4.

NOTE: Dissolving lye to 50% solution can sometimes be tricky. It is about the max load that the water can take. Be SURE the lye is completely dissolved; make sure it doesn't get too cool as it may start to re-crystallize at 50 °F. Lye solution will be safest to handle between 135 °F and 160 °F.

Phase 2: Measure and then Heat While Mixing
30.14 ounces Propylene Glycol
10.05 ounces Vegetable Glycerin
27.39 ounces 70% Sorbitol Solution
48.4 ounces Sodium Laureth Sulfate (SLES)

Phase 3: When Temperature of Phase 2 Reaches 140 °F Add and Mix
20.8 ounces Stearic Acid
9.7 ounces Myristic Acid

Phase 4: When temperature of Phase 3 reaches 165 °F slowly add lye solution in a thin slow stream from Phase 1 and mix. Intermitted (alternately stopping and starting again every few minutes) mix for about 20 minutes or until the soap base is transparent.

Phase 5: Discontinue mixing and let batch sit on heat for 1 hour at 165 °F.

Phase 6: Gently Stir in
4 ounces Triethanolamine (TEA)

Phase 7: For best results pour into soap molds between 150 °F and 155 °F.

Phase 8: Spray surface of soap with denatured alcohol to eliminate bubbles created while pouring warm soap into molds.

If for any reason you are not happy with the clarity or hardness of your batch you can reheat it and add 0.5% to 1% more TEA. However, oils and butters may impact the clarity of soap even with the addition of more TEA.

INCI Ingredient List
Sodium Laureth Sulfate, Propylene Glycol, Sorbitol, Sodium Stearate, Vegetable Glycerin, Sodium Myristate, Triethanolamine

Soap Notes: Attempted to removed TEA from the formula – resulted in soap base that lacked clarity.

Your Soap Notes:

Ultra Clear Melt & Pour Soap Base
10 lbs (160 ounces)

Two things make Melt and Pour Soap appear ultra clear – the color blue and a super clear base. Have you ever noticed that blocks of ultra clear soap have a blue hue to them? Well that is because there is always blue added to it. If there is yellow in your base this method won't work.

Phase Zero: Before starting any manufacturing project, sanitize the surface area you will be working on and all equipment, pots and utensils that you will use in the process. Refer to GMP section of the book for more detailed instructions.

Phase 1: Create Lye Solution by Mixing

Caution: Always wear safety gear, work in a ventilated area, use the appropriate vessel (stainless steel, Pyrex, heavy glass or plastic) and add the lye to the water and not vice versa. See Lye Safety Tips for more detailed information prior to doing Phase 1.

4.86 ounces De-ionized or Distilled Water
4.86 ounces Sodium Hydroxide

Clearly mark the lye mixture and set aside until asked for the lye solution in phase 4.

NOTE: Dissolving lye to 50% solution can sometimes be tricky. It is about the max load that the water can take. Be SURE the lye is completely dissolved; make sure it doesn't get too cool as it may start to re-crystallize at 50 °F. Lye solution will be safest to handle between 135 °F and 160 °F.

Phase 2: Measure and then Heat While Mixing
30.14 ounces Propylene Glycol
10.05 ounces Vegetable Glycerin
27.39 ounces 70% Sorbitol Solution
48.4 ounces Sodium Laureth Sulfate (SLES)

Phase 3: When Temperature of Phase 2 Reaches 140 °F Add and Mix
20.8 ounces Stearic Acid
9.7 ounces Myristic Acid

Phase 4: When temperature of Phase 3 reaches 165 °F slowly add lye solution in a thin slow stream from Phase 1 and mix. Intermitted (alternately stopping and starting again every few minutes) mix for about 20 minutes or until the soap base is transparent.

Phase 5: Discontinue mixing and let batch sit on heat for 1 hour at 165 °F.

Phase 6: Gently Stir in
4 ounces Triethanolamine (TEA)

Phase 7: Add and gently stir into the hot soap base 1 drop at a time of FD&C Blue Food Coloring (or blue of your choice).

Phase 8: For best results pour into soap molds between 150 °F and 155 °F.

Phase 9: Spray surface of soap with denatured alcohol to eliminate bubbles created while pouring warm soap into molds.

If for any reason you are not happy with the clarity or hardness of your batch you can reheat it and add 0.5% to 1% more TEA. However, oils and butters may impact the clarity of soap even with the addition of more TEA.

INCI Ingredient List
Sodium Laureth Sulfate, Propylene Glycol, Sorbitol, Sodium Stearate, Vegetable Glycerin, Sodium Myristate, Triethanolamine, FD&C Blue 1

Soap Notes: Attempted to removed TEA from the formula – resulted in soap base that lacked clarity.

Your Soap Notes:

White Melt & Pour Soap Base
10 lbs (160 ounces)

Phase Zero: Before starting any manufacturing project, sanitize the surface area you will be working on and all equipment, pots and utensils that you will use in the process. Refer to GMP section of the book for more detailed instructions.

Phase 1: Create Lye Solution by Mixing

Caution: Always wear safety gear, work in a ventilated area, use the appropriate vessel (stainless steel, Pyrex, heavy glass or plastic) and add the lye to the water and not vice versa. See Lye Safety Tips for more detailed information prior to doing Phase 1.

4. 75 ounces De-ionized or Distilled Water
4.75 ounces Sodium Hydroxide

Clearly mark the lye mixture and set aside until asked for the lye solution in phase 4.

NOTE: Dissolving lye to 50% solution can sometimes be tricky. It is about the max load that the water can take. Be SURE the lye is completely dissolved; make sure it doesn't get too cool as it may start to re-crystallize at 50 °F. Lye solution will be safest to handle between 135 °F and 160 °F.

Phase 2: Measure and then Heat While Mixing
29.75 ounces Propylene Glycol
11.45 ounces Vegetable Glycerin
31.25 ounces 70% Sorbitol Solution
47.6 ounces Bio-Terge 804

Phase 3: When Temperature of Phase 2 Reaches 140 °F Add and Mix
20.8 ounces Stearic Acid
9.7 ounces Myristic Acid

Phase 4: When temperature of Phase 3 reaches 165 °F slowly add lye solution in a thin slow stream from Phase 1 and mix. Intermitted (alternately stopping and starting again every few minutes) mix for about 20 minutes or until the soap base is transparent.

Phase 5: Discontinue mixing and let batch sit on heat for 1 hour at 165 °F.

Phase 6: In order to mix in Titanium Dioxide thoroughly without creating too many air bubbles, set your immersion stick blender on the bottom of your pot and mix in from there

3.2 ounces Titanium Dioxide

Phase 7: Discontinue mixing and let batch sit on heat for 5 minutes at 165 °F.

Phase 8: If you want to ensure that you get the hardest soap bar possible, add and gently stir into the hot soap base (155 °F and 165 °F)

1.6 ounces Myristic Acid
4.15 ounces Triethanolamine (TEA)

Phase 9: For best results pour into soap molds between 150 °F and 155 °F.

Phase 10: Spray surface of soap with denatured alcohol to eliminate bubbles created while pouring warm soap into molds.

If for any reason you are not happy with the clarity or hardness of your batch you can reheat it and add more TEA.

INCI Ingredient List
Propylene Glycol, Vegetable Glycerin, Sorbitol, Sodium Stearate, Sodium Myristate, Sodium C14-16 Olefin Sulfonate, Sodium Laureth Sulfate, Lauramide DEA, Titanium Dioxide.

INCI Ingredient List if you add the TEA
Propylene Glycol, Vegetable Glycerin, Sorbitol, Sodium Stearate, Sodium Myristate, Sodium C14-16 Olefin Sulfonate, Sodium Laureth Sulfate, Lauramide DEA, Triethanolamine, Titanium Dioxide.

Soap Notes: Re-melted a batch that turned out too soft and added 1% TEA – fixed the problem.

Your Soap Notes:

Basic Melt & Pour Soap Base with Oil/Butter Additives
10 lbs (160 ounces)

Because Melt and Pour Soap is made with so many surfactants and emulsifiers it is possible to add carrier oils to your formula. However both can cause clouding that may or may not be rectified with TEA.

Phase Zero: Before starting any manufacturing project, sanitize the surface area you will be working on and all equipment, pots and utensils that you will use in the process. Refer to GMP section of the book for more detailed instructions.

Phase 1: Create Lye Solution by Mixing

Caution: Always wear safety gear, work in a ventilated area, use the appropriate vessel (stainless steel, Pyrex, heavy glass or plastic) and add the lye to the water and not vice versa. See Lye Safety Tips for more detailed information prior to doing Phase 1.

4. 75 ounces De-ionized or Distilled Water
4.75 ounces Sodium Hydroxide

Clearly mark the lye mixture and set aside until asked for the lye solution in phase 4.

NOTE: Dissolving lye to 50% solution can sometimes be tricky. It is about the max load that the water can take. Be SURE the lye is completely dissolved; make sure it doesn't get too cool as it may start to re-crystallize at 50 °F. Lye solution will be safest to handle between 135 °F and 160 °F.

Phase 2: Measure and then Heat While Mixing
29.75 ounces Propylene Glycol
11.45 ounces Vegetable Glycerin
31.25 ounces 70% Sorbitol Solution
47.6 ounces Bio-Terge 804

Phase 3: When Temperature of Phase 2 Reaches 140 °F Add and Mix
20.8 ounces Stearic Acid
9.7 ounces Myristic Acid

Phase 4: When temperature of Phase 3 reaches 165 °F slowly add lye solution in a thin slow stream from Phase 1 and mix. Intermitted (alternately stopping and starting again every few minutes) mix for about 20 minutes or until the soap base is transparent.

Phase 5: Discontinue mixing and let batch sit on heat for 1 hour at 165 °F. Additives can impact the clarity of the finished product. If you want super clear soap skip ahead to Phase 8 and don't use additives.

Phase 6: Check for excessive fatty acids to ensure clarity of the batch. This can be done by one of the following two methods.

1. Pull a very small sample and allow it to cool completely. If when it is completely cooled (not warm at all) it is clear then your batch is ready to pour. You can speed up the cooling process by putting the sample in an artificially cooled area such as a refrigerator or freezer. If it appears cloudy then follow Phase 7.

2. Perform a cold water test similar to how you check hardness in candy. Fill a cup with cold water and drop about ½ tsp into the cold water. If the soap turns obviously cloudy follow Phase 7.

Phase 7: Add and GENTLY stir in
To add butters or oils at 1% add
1.65 ounces Butter or Oil

OR
To add butters or oils at 2% add
3.3 ounces Butter or Oil

OR
To add butters or oils at 3% add
4.95 ounces Butter or Oil

Phase 8: (only if phase 5 or 6 makes this step necessary) add and gently stir into the hot soap base
1.6 ounces Myristic Acid
4.15 ounces Triethanolamine (TEA)

Phase 9: For best results pour into soap molds between 150 °F and 155 °F.

Phase 10: Spray surface of soap with denatured alcohol to eliminate bubbles If for any reason you are not happy with the clarity of your batch you can reheat it and add more TEA, however oils and butters may impact the clarity of soap even with the addition of more TEA.

The following ingredient lists assume that you chose to use only one butter or oil. If you chose to use a combination of oils and/or butters than the TEA would fall before the list of additives.

INCI Ingredient List if you did not add TEA
Propylene Glycol, Vegetable Glycerin, Sorbitol, Sodium Stearate, Sodium Myristate, Sodium C14-16 Olefin Sulfonate, Sodium Laureth Sulfate, Lauramide DEA, (OIL OR BUTTER you added in with INCI name).

INCI Ingredient List if you did add TEA and added 1-2% Oil or Butter
Propylene Glycol, Vegetable Glycerin, Sorbitol, Sodium Stearate, Sodium Myristate, Sodium C14-16 Olefin Sulfonate, Sodium Laureth Sulfate, Lauramide DEA, Triethanolamine, (OIL OR BUTTER you added in with INCI name).

INCI Ingredient List if you did add TEA and added 3% Oil or Butter
Propylene Glycol, Vegetable Glycerin, Sorbitol, Sodium Stearate, Sodium Myristate, Sodium C14-16 Olefin Sulfonate, Sodium Laureth Sulfate, Lauramide DEA, (OIL OR BUTTER you added in with INCI name), Triethanolamine.

Soap Notes: Attempted to add various oils and butters before Phase 4 by using SAP values of additives – all batches above 1% failed. Batches at or below 1% failed for the most part. One batch with Shea Butter added before Phase 4 with the SAP value accounted for was acceptable, but cloudy. All batches with oils and butters added during Phase 7 passed.

Your Soap Notes:

High Sudz Melt & Pour Soap
10 lbs (160 ounces)

Phase Zero: Before starting any manufacturing project, sanitize the surface area you will be working on and all equipment, pots and utensils that you will use in the process. Refer to GMP section of the book for more detailed instructions.

Phase 1: Create Lye Solution by Mixing

Caution: Always wear safety gear, work in a ventilated area, use the appropriate vessel (stainless steel, Pyrex, heavy glass or plastic) and add the lye to the water and not vice versa. See Lye Safety Tips for more detailed information prior to doing Phase 1.

4.75 ounces De-ionized or Distilled Water
4.75 ounces Sodium Hydroxide

Clearly mark the lye mixture and set aside until asked for the lye solution in phase 4.

NOTE: Dissolving lye to 50% solution can sometimes be tricky. It is about the max load that the water can take. Be SURE the lye is completely dissolved; make sure it doesn't get too cool as it may start to re-crystallize at 50 °F. Lye solution will be safest to handle between 135 °F and 160 °F.

Phase 2: Measure and then Heat While Mixing
30.4 ounces Propylene Glycol
10.65 ounces Vegetable Glycerin
30.4 ounces 70% Sorbitol Solution
33.4 ounces Bio-Terge 804
14.58 ounces MPS Cocamidopropyl betaine

Phase 3: When Temperature of Phase 2 Reaches 140 °F Add and Mix
21.25 ounces Stearic Acid
9.7 ounces Myristic Acid

Phase 4: When temperature of Phase 3 reaches 165 °F slowly add lye solution in a thin slow stream from Phase 1 and mix. Intermitted (alternately stopping and starting again every few minutes) mix for about 20 minutes or until the soap base is transparent.

Phase 5: Discontinue mixing and let batch sit on heat for 1 hour at 165 °F.

Phase 6: Add and gently stir into the hot soap base
3.34 ounces Triethanolamine (TEA)

Phase 7: Due to the high foam potential of Cocamidopropyl betaine, MPS you may find a thin layer of white foam on top. Spray the top with denatured alcohol and bubbles will reduce. If some remains it is best to remove the layer of foam by skimming the top with a spoon and removing foamy layer.

Phase 8: For best results pour into soap molds between 150 °F and 155 °F.

Phase 9: Spray surface of soap with denatured alcohol to eliminate bubbles created while pouring warm soap into molds.

If for any reason you are not happy with the clarity or hardness of your batch you can reheat it and add more TEA, however oils and butters may impact the clarity of soap even with the addition of more TEA.

INCI Ingredient List if you did not add TEA
Propylene Glycol, Vegetable Glycerin, Sorbitol, Sodium Stearate, Sodium Myristate, Cocamidopropyl betaine, Sodium C14-16 Olefin Sulfonate, Sodium Laureth Sulfate, Lauramide DEA.

INCI Ingredient List if you did add TEA
Propylene Glycol, Vegetable Glycerin, Sorbitol, Sodium Stearate, Sodium Myristate, Cocamidopropyl betaine, Sodium C14-16 Olefin Sulfonate, Sodium Laureth Sulfate, Lauramide DEA, Triethanolamine.

Soap Notes: Attempted to use different Cocamidopropyl betaine – batch failed and was highly reactive in Phase 4 with temperatures rising to above 265 °F. Attempted to make an Ultra Clear version of this formula with the addition of TEA and blue coloring – batch failed because the base is too yellow resulting in a green soap.

Your Soap Notes:

Chapter 7

The Basics of Additives and Coloring

As I mentioned in the introduction, this book is about creating Melt and Pour Soap Base from Scratch. But I didn't want to leave you hanging with a big question mark asking, what do I do next with this Melt and Pour Soap base? Well, now the finished base is ready to scent, include additives and color. In this chapter I will cover the basics that can get you started with the new base that you made. More advanced techniques like layering, swirling, embedding and so forth needs to be saved for an entirely different book. A variety of books, tutorials, videos and websites teach a wide variety of Melt and Pour Soap techniques.

Melting Soap

The soap base must be heated in a suitable vessel. I recommend stainless steel for stove top or Pyrex for microwaving. Chop up your soap base into smaller chunks. This will make melting faster and with a more even temperature. You can melt it in the microwave for 30 seconds up to 1 minute at a time. When microwaving, cover with saran wrap to help trap moisture and reduce evaporation.

Heating should be done carefully to avoid over-heating it. If you overheat the soap, it can become discolored and the texture may be adversely affected. However, now that you know the inside scoop on Melt and Pour Soap Base recipes, you might know a trick or two to fix it. The addition of Propylene Glycol can make up for overheating and the loss of moisture by evaporation. Also, a discolored yellow hue may be caused by excessive evaporation and can be fixed with the addition of Propylene Glycol. The addition of TEA will help if clouding occurs.

Soap Molds

Use soap molds that are made of a suitable material that is able to handle soap temperatures between 135 °F and 155 °F. You can use flexible silicone molds, heavy duty molds, industrial molds and single cavity and trays molds.

Coloring Your Soap

The easiest method for coloring your soap is to use cosmetic grade, water based liquid colors. You can also use iron oxides, ultramarines, micas and natural ingredients with stable colors. Examples of cosmetic grade colorants are ones that have FD&C (Food, Drug and Cosmetic) or D&C (Drug and

Cosmetic) in the name. If you use cosmetic grade colorants remember, just a tiny bit of color goes a long way. Make sure you thoroughly stir FD&C and D&C colors into your hot melted soap base prior to pouring it into molds.

All iron oxides and ultramarines can be easily identified by their names and they are available in powder form. The easiest way to add iron oxides and ultramarines to your Melt and Pour Soap base is to saturate and mix them with a little denatured alcohol. Then add this blend into your melted soap base.

Micas come in a large variety of colors. They add glimmer, shimmer and fun to your soap. Micas often have other additives so be sure to read the ingredient list and fully disclose them on your finished product.

Natural Ingredients provide some fabulous hues and give your soap a beautiful appearance along with bonus side benefits. A few great examples include beta carotene, blue green algae and kelp, as well as green, pink, rhassoul and bentonite clay. Use a stick blender when adding heavy powders to fully incorporate them into your base before pouring. The best way to do this without creating too many bubbles is to use your blender to mix the clay into a slurry by taking ¼ of the soap you plan on using and then stir the slurry into the remaining soap. If you use clay you should add a preservative. Clay is dirt after all and when you add water your soap would become the perfect breeding grow for microorganisms.

A simple recipe for adding clay is:
16 oz Melt and Pour Soap base
0.16 oz Preservative Blend (from Essential Wholesale) or another paraben based blend
0.16 oz Clay of your choice

Mix Preservative Blend and clay together thoroughly and stir into melted soap.

Note: Only paraben based preservatives work as a broad spectrum preservative with clay when it is hydrated.

It is always good to do a test batch to see how stable your color will be. Some colors fade with exposure to light, others may react chemically with compounds in essential or fragrance oils. To test color stability, store one bar in a dark refrigerator, one bar in a room away from direct sunlight and one bar near a north facing window. It is good to find out early how your colors will stand up to the conditions they may face while in a store or with the consumer.

Scenting Your Soap
Adding essential oil or fragrance oil to your soap is super simple. The topic of

whether to use essential oils or fragrance oils is a bit more complicated so I've included the Addendum II, Scenting Your Soap :: Aromatherapy or Not? in order to go into the topic in more depth.

In general, you can scent your Melt and Pour soap between 1-3%. Certain essential oils and fragrance oils may discolor your soap immediately or over time. For instance, vanilla fragrance oil and lemongrass essential oil are well known for causing browning in your soap.

To add scent weigh the Melt and Pour Soap you will using. Multiply weight of Melt and Pour Soap base by either 0.1 (for 1%), 0.2 (for 2%) or 0.3 (for 3%) and then add that to your melted soap and stir thoroughly. If you chose fragrance oils make sure that you buy cosmetic grade and not candle fragrances.

Adding Exfoliants

Adding exfoliants and herbs can create a unique and natural appearance for your finished soap base. Popular exfoliants for soap include oatmeal, coffee, poppy seeds, whole herbs, loofah, jojoba beads, pumice and walnut powder. In order to best suspend your ingredients in your soap it is best to incorporate them by blending them into your soap base at the set up point temperature (125 °F) of your Melt and Pour Soap Base.

Pouring Your Soap into Molds

Depending on your soap mold, it is best to pour your finished soap between 135 °F and 155 °F. Pour your soap slowly and evenly into sanitized soap molds. Spray surface of soap with denatured alcohol to eliminate bubbles created while pouring warm soap into molds.

Unmolding Your Soap

In the ideal world you would allow your soap to completely cool for 12 to 24 hours and simply slip it out of the mold. But in today's fast paced world we all want our soap, and we want it now! If you can wait, simply allow your soap to cool completely for 12 to 24 hours and then apply pressure to the back of the mold and your soap should pop right out. If you don't want to wait you can use the freezer method. As soon as your soaps have set-up slightly, place the molds gently into the freezer. This is the easiest and quickest method to get the soap to release from a mold. You can leave the soap in freezer for approximately 10-20 minutes. Don't leave the soap in the freezer too long. Remove the mold from the freezer and allow the soap to sit for about 5 minutes. The soap will be easy to remove. Simply turn the mold over and apply pressure to the back. Be prepared to catch it or gently release the soap onto a hard surface.

Packaging Your Soap

When the soap bar has been removed from the mold and is at room temperature it should be wrapped to retain an attractive appearance. You can use shrink wrap, clear plastic food wrap used with a heat gun, cellophane bags, or other attractive plastic bags. Your soap should be stored at room temperature.

Labeling Your Soap

Remember your soap is a cosmetic and by law must be labeled appropriately. Use the ingredient lists I have provided with each recipe and don't forget to include any additives you add to your finished product. You must used INCI names for anything you add to your soap. For your convenience you can find complete list of INCI names on the Essential Wholesale website.

Chapter 8

Is it a Soap, Cosmetic or Drug?

Most of the recipes for Melt and Pour Soap Bases included in this book are, by the U.S. FDA definition, cosmetics and not of soaps. This means you are required to include a full International Nomenclature of Cosmetic Ingredients (INCI) ingredient list on every bar of soap and must follow all cosmetic regulations. (INCI ingredient list will be covered in Chapter 9.) It is very common to find Melt and Pour Soap, as well as true soaps, improperly labeled and containing drug claims. For that reason I am providing this information to help you navigate

"The FDA interprets the term "soap" to apply only when:
- The bulk of the nonvolatile matter in the product consists of an alkali salt of fatty acids and the product's detergent properties are due to the alkali-fatty acid compounds, and
- The product is labeled, sold, and represented solely as soap [21 CFR 701.20]." FDA

However, the majority of recipes in this book, and for that matter most Melt and Pour Soaps, do not meet the first standard, because the bulk of the product is not alkali salt and fatty acids.

"If a product intended to cleanse the human body does not meet all the criteria for soap, as listed above, it is either a cosmetic or a drug. For example:

If a product
- consists of detergents or
- primarily of alkali salts of fatty acids and
- is intended not only for cleansing but also for other cosmetic uses, such as beautifying or moisturizing, it is regulated as a cosmetic." FDA

The majority of the formulas in this book and all Melt and Pour Soaps consists of detergents and, by the FDA's definition, are a cosmetic and not soap. Detergents are essentially defatting agents which allows them to remove fats, lipids, dirt, make-up and debris from the surface of the skin. Detergents aren't bad; they just aren't by definition soap.

Understanding the Differences Between Drugs & Cosmetics

There is a fine line between drugs and cosmetics. It is important that as cosmetic companies we clearly stay on our side of the line and not walk the tight rope between the two definitions. Our job as cosmetic companies is to cleanse and promote beauty. We have plenty to do inside our own world without tinkering with the drug definitions. Whether you are making Melt and Pour Soap or true soap it is important to label your product correctly. It is common to make simple mistakes through the claims you make and turn your soap and/or cosmetic into a drug.

"If a product

- consists of detergents or
- primarily of alkali salts of fatty acids and
- is intended not only for cleansing but also to cure, treat, or prevent disease or to affect the structure or any function of the human body, it is regulated as a drug." FDA

For example, soaps that become a drug by the names they are given include: Acne Soap, Athlete's Foot Soap, and Anti-bacterial Soap.

What is a Cosmetic?

A cosmetic is defined in the Federal Food, Drug, Cosmetic Act, Section 201 (i) as being: Articles intended to be rubbed (*serums, moisturizers, etc.*), poured (*bubble baths, oils, etc.*), sprinkled (*body powders, bath powders, etc.*), or spray on (*body deodorant, perfumes, body mists, etc.*), introduced or otherwise applied to the human body or any part thereof for cleansing (*cleansers, exfoliants, etc.*), beautifying (*exfoliants, moisturizers, makeup, etc.*), promoting attractiveness (*makeup, perfumes, deodorants, etc.*) or altering the appearance (*cleansers, exfoliants, serums, moisturizers, makeup, etc.*)

Note: All *Italics* were added by me as examples and not official FDA comments.

Cosmetics exclude "soap". If your soap claims to be "cleansing, beautifying or moisturizing", it is a cosmetic and must be labeled appropriately.

Cosmetics are: not as regulated as drugs; require no pre-clearance by FDA; GMP is not required; have simple labeling regulations, and voluntary adverse effects reporting; cannot make any claims other than cosmetic usage even if it is accurate or nature's wonder "drug". The Cosmetic Legality Principle does not require pre-market approval or notification of products or ingredients; clearance of products safety or substantiation of product performance claims (*moisturizing, cleansing, deodorizing, etc.*); and mandatory establishment or product registration is currently voluntary.

The Manufacturer is responsible for making cosmetics safe and they must not be adulterated or misbranded. **Adulterated** is defined as harmful or injurious to user under customary conditions of use such as microbiology, unapproved color additive, chemical contaminant or prohibited ingredient. **Misbranded** is defined as when labeling is false or misleading; Package does not exhibit labeling information required by statute or regulation; Packaging not in compliance with 1970 Poison Prevention Packaging Act (PPPA).

What is a Drug?
A Drug is defined in Federal Food, Drug, Cosmetic Act, Section 201 (g) as being: Articles intended for use in the diagnosis, cure (*anti-wrinkle, anti-bacterial, anti-fungal, anti-acne etc.*), mitigation (*pain reliever, headache reducer, muscle relaxant, etc.*), treatment (*acne treatment, fungal treatment, wrinkle cures, psoriasis and eczema, anti-cancer treatments, etc.*) or prevention (*anti-scar, wrinkle cure, cancer prevention, anti-perspirant, etc.*), of disease. Articles (*other than food*) intended to affect the structure (*wrinkles, perspiration, scars, etc.*) or any function (*cell regeneration, collagen formation, etc.*) of the body.

Note: All *Italics* were added by me as examples and not official FDA comments.

Drugs: are highly regulated and require pre-clearance by FDA; GMP is required; have highly regulated labeling laws (i.e. Drug Facts); require reporting of all and any adverse effects known; can make proven, specific and tested claims that follow the monographs requirements. In the Drug Legality Principle a product meets the definition of drug if it complies with ALL requirements for drugs (even if it also meets the definition of cosmetic).

All cosmetics that meet the definition of a drug have to be registered and regulated by the FDA. Any product making claims such as, Sunscreens, Antibacterial Soap, Antidandruff Shampoo, Anti-Acne, Anti-Wrinkle, Antiperspirant, etc. are all considered drugs.

Your Products Intended Use Can Make Your Cosmetic a Drug

Example #1 Product Intended Use: Drug
A product with the following intended use is a drug: antiperspirant/deodorant (*stops perspirations*), dandruff shampoo (*treats dandruff*), sunscreen/suntan preparation (*prevents sunburn*), fluoride toothpaste (*prevents cavities*), and skin protectants (*helps heal cuts*).

Example #2 Products Intended Use: Cosmetic
A product with the following intended use is a cosmetic:

deodorant (*cover up odor*), shampoo (*cleanse hair*), suntan preparations (*moisturized while tanning*), toothpastes (*cleans teeth or freshens breath*), skin protectants (*moisturize skin*).

Notice that both the ingredients and the intended use of the product make a difference in whether it is considered a drug or a cosmetic. If an ingredient has a monograph it automatically makes a product a drug with the intended use as described in the monograph. The FDA has published monographs for OTC ingredients stating what ingredients can be used and their intended use. Using those ingredients in a product makes your cosmetic a drug. There are no if, ands or buts about it. If you use an ingredient with a monograph remember, if a product meets the definition of a drug, it must comply with ALL requirements for drugs (even if it also meets the definition of cosmetic).

Three Types of Claims that Can Cause Your Cosmetic to be a Drug

1. Claims that suggest physiological change. For instance, if you say "younger looking" rather than "younger" you are a cosmetic. If you say "removes" or "prevents" wrinkles, rather than "covers" you are a drug.

2. Claims that sound scientific. For instance, if you claim that your soaps are "Compounded in our laboratory under the most sterile conditions" or "If blemishes persist, see a doctor," you are a drug.

3. Claims that appear in an applicable OTC monograph. Sunscreen products, hormone products, acne, eczema, psoriasis, skin bleaching etc. Even implied claims by known effects of ingredients. For example, with skin bleaching products, the presence of many ingredients automatically make your product a drug.

Remember that even if a cosmetic has a drug action, it must qualify as a drug first and then a cosmetic.

Are You Transforming Your Cosmetic Into a Drug?
The trick is this, it doesn't matter whether the claim is true or not, it's whether the claim transforms the cosmetic into a drug. You might know that your soap helps lighten hyper-pigmentation, your ointment helps cure eczema, your serum irons out wrinkles, but as soon as you state or imply that fact on your label, in your literature, in any print advertisement, on your website, etc., you are placing your product into the drug category. Therefore, you must follow all drug regulations and need to present it to the FDA before it hits the market. You will also need to present case studies to the FDA to back up that claim. For

more information on this, go to The Center for Drug Evaluation and Research (CDER) Homepage.

Keep it Clean and Watch Your Advertising Claims

1. Environmental Claims: Claiming something is recyclable, even if true in your area, might not be true in other areas. For example, Polyethylene caps on your containers. There are only a few recycling outlets in the entire USA that recycle PE.

2. Made in America (or the USA Flag): Though your product might be made in the USA, the FTC/FDA requires all the ingredients originate and remain in the States, too.

3. Claiming to be an FDA approved product or an FDA approved facility

4. "Organic" Claims: If you are an organic certified entity, you will be notified of what you can place on your labels. If you are not then you can state "x% organic content" on the back of your packaging, but you can't state "organic" on the principal display panel. The verbiage must clearly state it is not certified.

5. "Natural" involves almost no regulation, however, integrity is recommended.

6. Product Claims Based on Ingredients: You can't advertise the effects of a known ingredient, all test studies must be done on the product itself.

7. Unsubstantiated endorsements (such as Celebrity Infomercials): Again, though a personal claim could be true, it might not necessarily be true for the average person.

8. Placing disclaimers like "Results may vary" or "Not typical for the average consumer." It is currently being noted that these disclaimers are not read, but rather the claims are just being heard. Therefore, disclaimers will probably go by the way side.

9. Using the term "cosmeceuticals": A product can be a drug, cosmetic or a combination of both following the rules of both standards. But the term "cosmeceutical" has no meaning under the law.

10. Mimicking: Just because you see another company making claims does not mean you should. If the FDA looks into your claim, you can't use another company's bad judgment as an excuse for your choices. And you don't know if the other company is actually complying with the law since much of it is behind the scenes, with the exception of "drug facts" on the label.

For a more detailed explanation of FDA labeling regulations I highly recommend the book Soap & Cosmetic Labeling, How to Follow the Rules and Regs Explained in Plain English by Marie Gale.

Chapter 9

The INCI Language of Cosmetic Ingredients Lists

All cosmetic ingredient lists must use INCI (International Nomenclature of Cosmetic Ingredients) names for all cosmetic ingredients in a finished product. The use of trade or common names is not allowed on cosmetic ingredient lists. INCI names are uniform scientific names and are mandated on the ingredient statement of every consumer personal care product.

INCI is an international designation for the declaration of the ingredients on the packaging of cosmetics. The use of INCI minimizes the language barriers that often hinder consumer understanding and international trade. The INCI names are allocated by the American Cosmetic Association, Personal Care Products Council and are used internationally. The adoption of INCI terminology ensures cosmetic ingredients are consistently listed using the same ingredient name from product to product.

In the U.S., the FDA requires all cosmetics include a listing of ingredients using the standardized INCI name for each ingredient in descending order. INCI ingredient names on product labels allow consumers to easily compare the ingredients between multiple products, using a common language. INCI ensures transparency in cosmetic ingredient disclosure.

INCI is required in America under the Food, Drug, and Cosmetic Act and the Fair Packaging and Labeling Act. In Canada INCI is required by Food and Drugs Act and Cosmetic Regulations. The declaration of the ingredients in accordance with the INCI system has been a legal requirement in the European Union since 1993. The declaration of ingredients in cosmetics with the INCI name is always required to be in descending order.

There are some that claim that "if you can't pronounce it, it can't be good for you" in reference to cosmetic ingredients. This statement from a banner at Natural Products Expo was made by the Environmental Working Group. It should take the award as the most uniformed, illogical statement ever made by a political action group. It simply proves they have no business attempting to be experts in the field of cosmetics and personal care that they attempt to be with their fatally flawed Skin Deep Database. If only they knew the simple fact that the cause for difficult to pronounce words in cosmetic labeling is due to internationally standardization to ensure consumer safety worldwide. I still can't say Butyrospermum parkii, but Shea Butter is as safe as ingredients come.

Whether you can pronounce the INCI term or not, the use of INCI nomenclature is the law. Always, always, always include any ingredients that you add to your Melt and Pour Soap base. This means if you add lemon essential oil to scent it, Yellow 5 to color it and poppy seeds as an exfoliant, all of the added ingredients must be included on the product ingredient list.

Chapter 10

Good Manufacturing Practices

Current Good Manufacturing Practice (GMP) guidelines are important for any size cosmetic or soap business to be familiar with. When proper cleanliness is not maintain your product can be deemed adulterated or misbranded, and you will be prohibited to sell it.

Following GMP is not required for cosmetic products, but the practices are worth knowing and working towards. No matter how much product you sell or how small your company is, now is a good time to implement as many GMP practices into your business as possible. Early on in our business my husband Dennis, insisted that we become GMP compliant. I knew it was the right thing to do but when I looked at all the GMP guidelines I was overwhelmed. But piece by piece we adopted GMP as normal and made it a habit.

If I had attempted to tackle the entire project all at once I would have thrown my hands up in frustration. We were growing fast and I was making all of the products myself. Dennis believed it was better to start the habits early so bad habits wouldn't inhibit our growth. He was right. We were not big when we started following GMP rules but he believed that we had to do business like the big boys in order to become a large business.

In this chapter I have addressed GMP guidelines in bite size chunks. How do you eat an elephant? That's right, one bite at a time. The entire GMP guidelines can be found on the FDA website. The following GMP Guidelines/Inspection Checklist is provided by the FDA. I have provided helpful hints throughout the FDA guidelines from what we learned growing our home business into a fully GMP compliant business. Becoming the Certified Organic Processor and Handler that we are today much easier to accomplish because we were already GMP compliant.

The following cosmetic establishment instructions, excerpted from FDA's Inspection Operations Manual, may serve as guidelines for effective self-inspection. Take advantage of the fact that the FDA publishes their Inspection Operations Manual by putting on your white gloves to "inspect" your facility. All quotes are from the FDA's website and non quotes are my tips to help you make your facility GMP compliant. The numbering of the tips corresponds to the FDA excerpts.

Guidelines

1. Building and Facilities. Check whether:

> **a.** "Buildings used in the manufacture or storage of cosmetics are of suitable size, design and construction to permit unobstructed placement of equipment, orderly storage of materials, sanitary operation, and proper cleaning and maintenance."

> **Building Suitability Tips:** You may need to designate one part of your kitchen or house as "manufacturing space only" and guard that space with your life. Of course that is not required as long as the space, whether temporary or permanent, is always clean before you begin production.

> **b.** "Floors, walls and ceilings are constructed of smooth, easily cleanable surfaces and are kept clean and in good repair."

> **Counters, Walls, Ceilings and Floors Tips:** This does not mean you have to remodel your entire kitchen, but your designated area needs to have easy to wipe off surfaces. For example:
> **Counters:** Stainless steel, laminate, corian, staron are all non-porous, smooth surfaces suitable for keeping clean and in good repair. Tiles with grout, wood and other porous materials are not ideal for this area.
> **Walls/Ceilings:** 4x8 sheets of Fiberglass Reinforced Panel (FRP) are FDA accepted sanitary wall liners. FRP panels are available at Home Depot for approximately $32 per panel.
> **Floors:** Vinyl floors are best for cleaning up. Also having a clean kitchen is okay to as long as the product cannot be adulterated by its surroundings.

> **c.** "Fixtures, ducts and pipes are installed in such a manner that drip or condensate does not contaminate cosmetic materials, utensils, cosmetic contact surfaces of equipment, or finished products in bulk."

> **Fixtures, Ducts and Pipes Tips:** This may seem obvious, but look up while you are in the midst of a hot cook. Check out all the surfaces the steam reaches. Every surface should be cleaned religiously and be painted with a washable paint if the surface is porous. If it is a painted surface it must not flake or hold moisture. An example of a good washable paint is Gliddon Evermore super washable flat latex paint for highly washable surfaces. Most brands have a paint that is designed to create an

easy to wash off surface. You can also prime or seal any porous surface prior to painting.

d. "Lighting and ventilation are sufficient for the intended operation and comfort of personnel."

Lighting and Ventilation Tips: Be certain that you can clearly see what you are doing. Make sure all areas are well illuminated so you can see if you're working in a clean area. If you are using powders, minerals, lye or essential oils you should make sure the area is ventilated as well.

e. "Water supply, washing and toilet facilities, floor drainage and sewage system are adequate for sanitary operation and cleaning of facilities, equipment and utensils, as well as to satisfy employee needs and facilitate personal cleanliness."

Water Systems Tips: When we moved into our second building we discovered the walk through we did with our landlord was not completely accurate. It wasn't until we brought in a plumber to install a three-hole sink that we discovered the plumbing and drainage from the building wasn't sufficient to add the all important water source. The year and a half that we spent in that building presented many challenges. The landlord simply did not know it wouldn't be possible. So if you are moving into a building and it needs any work, including ventilation, electricity, plumbing or any other important modification, make sure you bring in an expert before signing the lease.

Having a clean, safe and well lit facility is an important step in the manufacturing of cosmetics. Two recent issues that the FDA has had to address with companies have been related to cleanliness. The peanut butter recall is one and the hand sanitizer recall is another. The best way to avoid a recall is to go above and beyond in the care of your work space.

2. Equipment. Check whether:

a. "Equipment and utensils used in processing, holding, transferring and filling are of appropriate design, material and workmanship to prevent corrosion, buildup of material, or adulteration with lubricants, dirt or sanitizing agent."

Appropriate Designs Tips: Even when you have the right equipment, if it isn't properly maintained, you are wasting your money. It is vital to use the right equipment, maintain it, clean it and log it all. Creating logs not only gives you a bird's eye view of your own systems but also provides a record of your compliance with GMP regarding equipment.

Depending on what you are manufacturing, the right equipment for one company might not be the right equipment for another. In general, stainless steel is best for most equipment. The key to cleaning equipment and not transferring contamination from one batch to another is to use non-porous materials. Once you invest in the right equipment maintain it, log it, maintain it, log it, maintain it, and log it!

b. "Utensils, transfer piping and cosmetic contact surfaces of equipment are well-maintained and clean and are sanitized at appropriate intervals."

Maintenance Tips: The key to proper maintenance, cleaning and sanitizing is to log it. It might all seem redundant but the extra step of logging it is worth it. There is a difference between cleaning and sanitizing. We wash all of our utensils with warm water and soap, rinse, sanitize and dry. Then, when we put that same utensil into use, we sanitize if it again. Our sanitizing step is to wipe down every surface with denatured alcohol. We sanitize right before use in case any contaminate is transferred onto the surface. It might be over kill but I'd rather be "over the top clean" than contaminate a product, because recalls can be expensive.

c. "Cleaned and sanitized portable equipment and utensils are stored and located, and cosmetic contact surfaces of equipment are covered, in a manner that protects them from splash, dust or other contamination."

Storage and Locations Tips: If you are operating out of your home, make sure you have a dedicated area that is not mixed with personal items. Depending on the size of your equipment, there are many options for storage. Just make sure there is no cross contamination caused by splash, dust or any other possible contamination. Treat your equipment and utensils like precious treasures.

3. Personnel. Check whether:

    a. "The personnel supervising or performing the manufacture or control of cosmetics has the education, training and/or experience to perform the assigned functions."

> **Education and Training Tips:** Create Standard Operating Procedures (SOP) so there will never be an "I wasn't told that" or an "Oops I forgot" step. SOPs are a standardized set of instructions that you create for every aspect of QC, manufacturing, filling, labeling, logging, packaging, shipping and any other step your product goes through from the time the ingredients arrive to the moment the finished product is shipped out of your building. No step is too mundane to include in your SOPs. You cannot purchase a set of SOPs to fit your situation. You must create your own SOP that best suit the needs of your company.
>
> The SOP should be a written document including all the instructions with detailed steps and processes simple enough that a 5th grader could do it - with the same results you would get yourself. The steps should be without any variation or change. In this way, you will always get the same results whether you make it yourself or someone follows your SOP to complete the task.
>
> Every employee should be thoroughly trained on your SOP and their training should be documented. If your SOPs are updated or changed, your employees should be retrained and that training documented. The purpose of the SOP is not to make the job harder, but to make it easier and standardized. Imagine that someday you could go on vacation and your company would run without you. The SOPs get you one step closer to that dream.

    b. "Persons coming into direct contact with cosmetic materials, finished products in bulk or cosmetic contact surfaces, to the extent necessary to prevent adulteration of cosmetic products, wear appropriate outer garments, gloves, hair restraints etc., and maintain adequate personal cleanliness."

> **Appropriate Garments Tips:** There is nothing sexier than a hairnet and pair of gloves! Get over feeling silly and make a habit of wearing them. It is the easiest step of all. You can buy them at Costco or Cash and Carry. They are inexpensive and simple. Gloves and hairnets have become so common for me that when I recently visited a large food manufacturing facility and watched someone touch the food without gloves I nearly fainted. Germs

live on our hands and are easily transferred to products. I recently read there are 50,000 bacteria per square inch of skin that are harmless on your skin but what about in your product?

c. "Consumption of food or drink, or use of tobacco is restricted to appropriately designated areas."

Food Tips: If you are in your kitchen this is hard to adhere to but you have to make it a habit to protect the area you work in from cross contamination of food. Pretend that zone, or the time period in which you use the area, is a sanctuary and guard it.

4. Raw Materials. Check whether:

a. "Raw materials and primary packaging materials are stored and handled in a manner which prevents their mix-up, contamination with microorganisms or other chemicals, or decomposition from exposure to excessive heat, cold, sunlight or moisture."

Raw Materials and Primary Packaging Tips: Make sure you store all ingredients and finished products at the proper temperature for that particular product. Not all things should be stored in the refrigerator! Have you ever noticed the condensation in your mayonnaise jar. The same thing can happen to your ingredients or cosmetics. That is why mayo contains EDTA but your raw ingredient does not always have it. Sometimes we get calls regarding clouding of oils that were stored in the fridge and that is because the condensation has fallen into the oil. Also the condensation can grow mold and then contaminate your product. If you use the fridge do not use the door panels. And it is best to have a dedicated fridge that won't be opened and closed a zillion times per day.
Don't store anything in the sunlight. Even if you are extracting St. John's Wort in oil and the sunlight is needed to get the red color, make sure every evening it is opened and the condensation wiped off. Nothing else has any reason to be in the sun.

Find a room that you can maintain a steady room temperature to store all ingredients. The garage is a very poor choice. One day in a warm area can be equal to approximately 4 days of the product's life and excessive heat accelerates the effect. 40 degrees C (104 degrees F) is commonly used for accelerated shelf life testing and you don't want to be accelerating your shelf life while you are storing your products.

Don't store your food items with your supplies. Every incoming ingredient should be logged, QC'd and marked with a label. At Essential Wholesale we micro test every single incoming ingredient we bring in for resale or manufacturing. It might be too big of a step right now for you to test every incoming ingredient, but you can rest assured every ingredient and every product has been micro tested at Essential Wholesale before it ever reaches your door. A finished product from Essential Wholesale represents many micro tests as each ingredient is micro tested prior to use, and the finished product is micro tested prior to sale.

We had an incident where aloe juice contaminated a well preserved product and destroyed it: Our customer wanted to use their own aloe juice instead of ours. We were already in the practice of micro testing all of our incoming ingredients so we were shocked when the finished product we had made with the customer's juice failed the micro test. This was several years ago and we were not in the practice of micro testing a customer's incoming ingredients, but everything changed from that day forward. We had to throw away five gallons of very expensive product that had been scented with $235 worth of Jasmine Absolute. Trust me when I say we learned a hard lesson and never manufactured with a single untested ingredient again!

b. "Containers of materials are closed, and bagged or boxed materials are stored off the floor."

Containers and Storage Tips: Storing on the floor is a common food and cosmetic violation and it is simple to avoid with low shelving or even cut a pallet to fit the area. Don't just roll a bag up and assume it is closed. Clip it, change packaging, and put it in bins from Home Depot. You need to protect your ingredients from the moisture in the air, the dust floating everywhere, and critters that want to check out what you have in there.

c. "Containers of materials are labeled with respect to identity, lot identification and control status."

Log and Label Tip: Do this as the ingredients come in and keep a log. Document it, log it, document it, and log it. Am I starting to sound like a broken record yet? Logs can be paperless by creating an Excel spreadsheet that includes all of your logs in one place.

d. "Materials are sampled and tested or examined in conformance with procedures assuring the absence of contamination with filth, microorganisms, or other extraneous substances, to the extent necessary to prevent adulteration of finished products. Pay particular attention to materials of animal or vegetable origin and those used in the manufacture of cosmetics by cold processing methods with respect to contamination with filth or microorganisms."

Sampling and Testing Tip: Visual inspection can work for some of these parameters. Otherwise, depend on your supply source or add micro testing of your incoming ingredients to the steps that you usually take. If you buy from Essential Wholesale you can count on us having all the QC and micro testing documents on every ingredient. With a lot number we can find every detail about an ingredient from when it arrived, when it was micro tested, when it passed, visual inspection, aroma, and many other variations along with a sample of the lot. We take QC seriously on all incoming and outgoing ingredients and finished product.

e. "Materials not meeting acceptance specifications are properly identified and controlled to prevent their use in cosmetics."

Failing Specifications Tip: Destroy or return everything that doesn't pass your QC tests and document the process. If you have to destroy or return a product or ingredient you must log it. This will keep you GMP compliant and also can be used by your tax preparer as a business loss.

5. Production. Check whether manufacturing and control have been established and that written instructions, i.e. formulations, processing, transfer and filling instructions, in-process control methods etc. are being maintained. Determine whether such procedures require that:"

Document, Document, Document! Log it, Log it, Log it! Create SOPs, train your employees on SOPs and implement SOPs! Your formulas should include methodology that spell out your SOPs for that product and include every step from incoming raw ingredient QC; to storage of raw ingredients; to manufacturing; methodology; filling; labeling; packing; and shipping. The Standard Operating Procedure must be clearly written, followed, documented and consistently.

a. "The equipment for processing, transfer and filling the utensils and the containers for holding raw and bulk materials are clean, in good repair and in sanitary condition."

> **Condition of Equipment Tip:** GMP for Equipment should follow all stages of your product development. That means the equipment for manufacturing, the equipment you use to transfer and fill, are as clean as the containers which hold the raw materials.

b. "Only approved materials are used."

> **Only Approved Materials Tip:** Use your QC Log for incoming materials to keep track of materials you approved and materials that fail QC. Every ingredient or product that fails QC must be added to a Destruction Log that keeps records of what happens to the materials that fail QC. Indicate which materials were rejected and sent back to the supplier or destroyed.

c. "Samples are taken, as appropriate, during and/or after processing, transfer or filling for testing for adequacy of mixing or other forms of processing, absence of hazardous microorganisms or chemical contaminants, and compliance with any other acceptance specification."

> **Samples Tips:** You should take a sample of every incoming and outgoing product that you QC and retain the sample. We retain all of our samples for 3 years. You must also retain all testing documents and QC logs. When you buy an ingredient or finished product from Essential Wholesale put the Lot # into your incoming records and that will tie your records to our records to complete the chain of QC Logs. We have records on every raw ingredient and finished products we sell and they meet every one of the standards listed above for our company and yours.

d. "Weighing and measuring of raw materials is checked by a second person, and containers holding the materials are properly identified."

> **Weighing and Measuring Tips:** For a one man show this is a huge hurdle. We are working towards having this changed or waved for small businesses in our efforts with the FDA. One idea that might work for your small company is to pre-measure, label and store your ingredients when you have another person with you that can check your measurements. For instance, you receive 50 lbs of shea butter and you only use 10 lbs of shea butter per batch of soap, with a fellow soaper, friend or family member can be present to check measurements and break down the shea butter into five 10 lb packages. Label, log, and store the shea for

future batches. Do the same with as many ingredients as possible. If you have more than one person at your company this is not as big of a hurdle but can still be inconvenient. Also go the extra mile and get your scale calibrated to ensure your scale is accurate at all times.

e. "Major equipment, transfer lines, containers and tanks are used for processing, filling or holding cosmetics. All are identified to indicate contents, batch designation, control status and other pertinent information."

Know your Steps: Carry the same lot number and documentation all the way through every step of manufacturing. You should be able to clearly identify from a label on a batch of product at any phase of the production what it is, the lot number, what stage of manufacturing it is in, whether it has passed QC and where it is going from there.

f. "Labels are examined for identity before labeling operations to avoid mix-up."

Avoid Mislabeling Tip: Check your labeling, double check and check again. There is nothing worse than labeling cucumber lotion as coffee shampoo...!

g. "The equipment for processing, holding, transferring and filling of batch is labeled regarding identity, batch identification and control status."

Equipment Identifying Batch: As your product moves from the equipment that you process it in, hold it, transfer and fill it should be clearly marked with the product name, batch number and control status of that product at that moment.

h. "Packages of finished products bear permanent code marks."

Permanent Code Mark Tip: You need to keep track of a product from start to finish. The finished product should have a permanent code mark that can help you identify the batch and logs associated with it.

i. "Returned cosmetics are examined for deterioration or contamination."

> **Returned Products Tip:** If a product is returned to you, it should not be only thrown away even if the customer didn't like it. A returned product is an opportunity to evaluate how the product stands up under real life conditions.

6. Laboratory Controls. Check whether:

    a. "Raw materials, in-process samples and finished products are tested or examined to verify their identity and determine their compliance with specifications for physical and chemical properties, microbial contamination, and hazardous or other unwanted chemical contaminants."

> **Compliance with Specifications of Physical and Chemical Properties Tips:** Does that statement terrify you? There are some easy steps you can add to aid in laboratory controls in your company. These are just examples that you can modify depending on your needs.
>
> **Tips for creating your own _incoming_ Quality Control Log:**
> 1. Name of Product
> 2. Supplier Name
> 3. Lot Number from Supplier
> 4. Lot Number assigned by your company (if not the same as from supplier)
> 5. Date Received
> 6. Invoice Number from supplier
> 7. Quantity receiving into inventory
> 8. QC checked by
> 9. Date & Time of QC
> 10. Colour of the product - indicate if there is any variance (which is common in natural products)
> 11. Micro test Results - either micro test in house or if you received it from Essential Wholesale indicate "passed as per EW". Nothing leaves our building unless it has passed the micro test so you are guaranteed we have a record of every product passing micro tests.
> 12. pH can be measured with pH strips or if your products come from Essential Wholesale you can indicate "EW" because we have records if it is ever needed.
> 13. Scent - indicate if there is a variance and describe the aroma
> 14. Viscosity - describe it and indicate any variance

15. Texture - describe it and indicate any variance
16. Approved or Rejected
17. Explanation and course of action if rejected

Tips for creating your own *finished* goods Quality Control Log:
1. Product name
2. Batch Size
3. Order number if production is to fill a specific order
4. End user to indicate if it is for stock, private label customer, specific store
5. Compounded by
6. Measurements Checked by
7. Compounding Date
8. Sample pulled & by whom
9. Micro test Results - either micro test in house or if you received it from Essential Wholesale indicate "passed as per EW". Nothing leaves our building unless it has passed micro testing so you are guaranteed we have a record of every product passing micro tests.
10. Viscosity, describe it and indicate any variance (unless you have a viscometer)
11. pH
12. QC'd by
13. Lot # Assigned
14. Filling Date
15. Filled by
16. Parent Product # (if using a finished product to make other products - example if you make a product that you scent various ways to make other products)
17. Child Product Name
18. Child Product Lot # Assigned
19. Product Retest Date

b. "Reserve samples of approved lots or batches of raw materials and finished products are retained for the specified time period, are stored under conditions that protect them from contamination or deterioration, and are retested for continued compliance with established acceptance specifications."

Reserve Samples Tips: Make sure you hold onto all of your samples of every batch of product you make. The labeling on the lot sample should make it simple to find the paperwork attached to that lot number. Store your lot samples under similar conditions that your product will have in the stores. Don't hang onto them in the garage where they are sure to be destroyed.

c. "The water supply, particularly the water used as a cosmetic ingredient, is tested regularly for conformance with chemical-analytical and microbiological specifications."

> **Water Supply Tip:** Your water source is critical. At Essential Wholesale we take our water source seriously because even if you take every step to ensure clean raw materials, contaminated water can destroy your product. You should use de-ionized water or distilled water to manufacture your products, not tap water.

d. "Fresh as well as retained samples of finished products are tested for adequacy of preservation against microbial contamination, which may occur user reasonably foreseeable condition of storage and consumer use."

> **Testing Tips:** Even when you have your products tested at production, real life conditions can be the best indicator of a successful preservation system.

7. Records. Check whether control records are maintained of:

a. Raw materials and primary packaging materials, documenting disposition of rejected materials.

b. Manufacturing of batches, documenting the:
   i. Kinds, lots and quantities of material used.
   ii. Processing, handling, transferring, holding and filling.
   iii. Sampling, controlling, adjusting and reworking.
   iv. Code marks of batches and finished products.

c. Finished products, documenting sampling, individual laboratory controls, test results and control status.

d. Distribution, documenting initial interstate shipment, code marks and consignees."

> **Records Tips:** Going through all the steps to be GMP compliant is essential but you also must keep records of it all. That is why I've been repeating myself with log it, log it, and log it! You should always be able to find your documents, logs, product sample, and finished product. The trick is to follow all the other steps of GMP and keep accurate records on your compliance

every day. You can't back log this kind of data; it must all be kept along the way.

8. Labeling. Check whether the labels of the immediate and outer container bear:

   a. On the principal display panel:
     i. In addition to the name of the product, the statements of identity and net contents,
     ii. The statement "Warning--The safety of this product has not been determined" if the safety of the respective product has not adequately been substantiated. Determine whether and what toxicological and/or other testing the firm has conducted to substantiate the safety of its products. See 21 CFR 740.10.

   b. On the information panel:
     i. The name and address of the firm manufacturing the product or introducing it into interstate commerce.
     ii. The list of ingredients (only on outer container) if intended for sale or customarily sold to consumers for consumption at home.
     iii. The warning statement(s) required at 21 CFR 740.11, 740.12 and 740.17.
     iv. Any other warning statement necessary or appropriate to prevent a health hazard. Determine the health hazard or their basis for a warning statement.
     v. Any direction for safe use of product."

Labeling Tip: The best investment you can make to ensure proper labeling and avoid misbranding is the book, Soap & Cosmetic Labeling, How to Follow The Rules and Regs, Explained in Plain English by Marie Gale. There are too many details for a single blog post on labeling and Marie Gale literally wrote the book on Soap and Cosmetic labeling.

9. Complaints. Check whether the firm maintains a consumer complaint file and determine:

   a. The kind and severity of each reported injury and the body part involved.

b. The product associated with each injury, including the manufacturer and code number.

c. The medical treatment involved, if any, including the name of the attending physician.

d. The name(s) and location(s) of any poison control center, government agency, physician's group etc., to whom formula information and/or toxicity data are provided."

Complaints Tips: We haven't had or known anyone who has had any complaints of bodily harm from cosmetics. But you should have protocol in place so you or your employees know exactly what to do if you ever receive such a compliant. It is easier to take the correct steps if you are prepared for the worst.

Create a log (that you pray always stays empty) that includes: Customers name, date of injury, date of call, kind of injury, body part injured, product that caused injury, lot number of product, medical treatment needed, name of the attending physician, hospital, whether you were contacted by poison control or a government agency. You never want to get this call but it is best to be prepared. You might want to designate who should take the call as well.

All of these GMP tips might have seemed a bit overwhelming for you, but don't disregard them altogether. Think big, dream big and aim high by working as many of the GMP compliance guidelines into your working business as possible.

Chapter 11

Soap Notes and Formulation in Progress

"Natural" Melt & Pour Soap Base In-Progress-Formula – 6 lbs (96 ounces)

This recipe is only included for information and for those who love to experiment. It is meant to be a jumping off point for those who want to formulate a "natural" or mostly natural melt and pour soap base. I have had hit and miss success with this recipe and since this form of soap isn't the focus of this book I ran out of time to allow it to cure enough times to have a sure-fire recipe for your use. But I know many are born to research, develop and experiment and I wanted to provide you with my notes to give you a head start in your journey. This recipe assumes you are already an experienced soapmaker and know how to make transparent soap.

Phase Zero: Before starting any manufacturing project, sanitize the surface area you will be working on and all equipment, pots and utensils that you will use in the process. Refer to GMP section of the book for more detailed instructions.

Phase 1: Create Lye Solution by Mixing

Caution: Always wear safety gear, work in a ventilated area, use the appropriate vessel (stainless steel, Pyrex, heavy glass or plastic) and add the lye to the water and not vice versa. See Lye Safety Tips for more detailed information prior to doing Phase 1.

10 ounces De-ionized or Distilled Water
4.8 ounces Sodium Hydroxide

Clearly mark the lye mixture and set aside until asked for the lye solution in phase 3.

Phase 2: Measure and Heat Oils
14.6 ounces Palm Oil
6.6 ounces Coconut Oil
10 ounces Castor Oil

Phase 3: Check Temperatures and Combine Phases 1 and 2

Caution: Always wear safety gear, work in a ventilated area, use the appropriate vessel (stainless steel, Pyrex, heavy glass or plastic) (stainless steel, Pyrex, heavy glass or plastic) and add the lye to the water and not vice versa. See Lye Safety Tips for more detailed information prior to doing Phase 3.

When the lye solution falls to between 135 °F and 145 °F and the oil is between 135 °F and 145 °F slowly add lye solution in a thin slow stream from Phase 1 and into Phase 2 Oils. Stir continuously and steadily with a stick blender. The mixture will thicken and "trace" in 3-5 minutes.

Phase 4: Maintain Heat and Cover

Keep the mixture hot for 1 hour over low heat and cover with lid. Stir occasionally. The temperature should rise to 170 °F to 180 °F. The soap will become transparent as it passes through the gel phase.

At the end of an hour check to see if the surface of the soap is translucent. Mix the soap thoroughly with a hand mixer and work to incorporate any soap from the edges of the pot back into the mixture.
Cover the soap for another hour on low.

Phase 5: Check to see if the soap is neutral to ensure clarity of the batch. This can be done by adding a small sample to a glass of water. If the soap is neutral it will dissolve.

Phase 6: Remove from heat, add and mix into soap base

Caution: Alcohol is very flammable. Never use around an open flame or heat source. Know where your fire extinguisher is at all times when working with alcohol. Have adequate ventilation in your work area. Use a large enough pot to allow for alcohol to be mixed into the product without causing the soap to overflow. Store alcohol in a break-proof container away from an open flame.

11.2 ounces Denatured Alcohol
3.65 ounces Kosher Vegetable Glycerin

Phase 7: Mix thoroughly, return to heat on medium and cover for 30 minutes. Do not leave the pot unsupervised to ensure that it doesn't overheat and overflow.

Stir mixture and check the temperature. When soap reaches 160 °F continue to stir intermitted (alternately stopping and starting again every few minutes) for the next 15-30 minutes until the soap is fully dissolved into the alcohol and glycerin.

Phase 8: 70% Sorbitol Solution

14.1 ounces 70% Sorbitol Solution

The Sorbitol will assist in transparency; it replaces sugar water in traditional clear soap recipes.

Phase 9: Add and Mix
21.2 ounces Propylene Glycol
Propylene Glycol is required in order for any formula of soap to re-melt and pour. I have already tested replacing propylene glycol with glycerin, Sorbitol, hyaluronic acid and other more natural and label friendly ingredients. It doesn't work in this recipe or any of the others.

Phase 10: For best results pour into soap molds between 150 °F and 155 °F.

Phase 11: Spray surface of soap with denatured alcohol to eliminate bubbles created while pouring warm soap into molds. Allow to cure for 2 weeks.

This recipe qualifies as a true soap. An ingredient deck is not required. If you want to use an ingredient list it could be stated in more than one way.

What goes into the pot format:

Propylene Glycol, Elaeis guineensis (Palm) Oil, Sorbitol, Ethanol, Ricinus Communis (Castor) Oil, Aqua, Cocos nucifera (Coconut), Sodium Hydroxide, Glycerin

What comes out of the pot format:

Propylene glycol, sodium palmate, sorbitol, sodium castorate, sodium cocoate, water, glycerin

You will often see Natural Melt and Pour Soap bases that do not include propylene glycol in the ingredient list. My guess is that they are calling it a "processing aid" or since it is not a cosmetic they have chosen not to disclose all the ingredients.

Soap Notes:
This recipe has worked perfectly on most occasions for at least one re-melt and pour. It has on one occasion turned out cloudy re-melting. Remember this is a starting point recipe and you are free to work your soapmaking magic from here.

I have had success melting the above formula down and mixing it 50:50 with the Basic Melt and Pour Soap. The next step I plan on taking with this recipe is to add Stearic Acid and Myristic Acid into Phase 2.

My failures with "Natural" Melt & Pour Soap Base In-Progress-Formula:
Adding Myristic Acid in Phase 9
Adding Myristic Acid and TEA in Phase 9
Adding TEA in Phase 9
Replacing Propylene Glycol with Glycerin
Replacing Propylene Glycol with Hyaluronic Acid
Removing Propylene Glycol

Addendum I

My Little Soap Box

Cocamidopropyl betaine an excellent example of how information about cosmetic ingredients has been misused by organizations with an agenda. For example, according to Skin Deep, Cocamidopropyl betaine is rated as a moderate hazard due to: "Violations, Restrictions & Warning, Allergies/immunotoxicity, Contamination Concerns, Ecotoxicology." However, the safety data on Cocomidopropyl betaine that it isn't a hazard at all. Below is a review of each of the points given to Cocoamidopropyl betaine and the scientific facts that dispute the rating.

Violations, Restrictions & Warnings

According the Skin Deep's point system Cocamidopropyl betaine is given 1 point because Skin Deep referenced a CIR Expert Panel finding of: "Determined safe for use in cosmetics, subject to concentration or use limitations. Safe for use in cosmetics with some qualifications." The CIR Expert Panel determined that "Cocamidopropyl betaine is safe as used in rinse-off products" but because it gave some qualifications Cocamidopropyl betaine in leave on products it was given a bad point on the Skin Deep rating system.

A closer look at what the "restrictions" are voids this point against the ingredient altogether. From the CIR Expert Panel findings here is the actual finding, "Safe with qualifications" and the qualifications are, "safe as used in rinse-off products; but 3% or less in leave-on products." Cocamidopropyl betaine is only used in rinse-off products! It is completely proven safe in rinse-off products. There is no reason to be alarmed about using Cocamidopropyl betaine in your shampoo, shower gel, hand soap, cleanser or any rinse-off product. The products the Skin Deep refers to that contain Cocamidopropyl betaine are all rinse-off products.

There is absolutely no sound reason for Cocamidopropyl betaine to be given a point for violations, restrictions and warnings. But it certainly does sound alarming that it has been given this point! Turn off this alarm because it is false. With that proven Cocamidopropyl betaine should be at a rating of 4, but let's continue on to see if the other scores hold water.

Allergies/Immunotoxicity

Allergies are probably one of the most interesting topics of them all. Really every single ingredient used in food, cosmetics, pharmaceuticals, tobacco, and found in nature should get this point if we are giving it out. There is nothing on earth that is completely allergen free for everyone. I suffer from severe allergies so I understand the concern over the topic. The potential for causing allergies in someone is in everything on earth. With that said, what I found really interesting about this topic in relation to Cocamidopropyl betaine getting a point is there have been studies done on the original studies that were not reported on Skin Deep.

J. Edward Hunter and Joseph F. Fowler Jr. found that, "Cocamidopropyl betaine (CAPB) is a mild surfactant used in shampoos, conditioners, body washes, and other personal-care products. Several recently published case reports have suggested that CAPB may be a skin sensitizer. A 6-week product-use study was conducted to determine whether subjects with previous positive patch tests to CAPB could use personal-care products (prototype hair shampoo, liquid hand soap, and body wash) with this surfactant without problems. Post-study patch testing suggested that amidoamine, a material used in the synthesis of CAPB and a contaminant of CAPB preparations, is a likely sensitizer. However, patch testing did not rule out the possibility that CAPB itself may be an allergen to a small number of pre-sensitized individuals. It is recommended that CAPB with minimal levels of contamination be used for the formulation of personal-care products."

In plain English they found that a Cocamidopropyl betaine that had amindoamine left over in it from the chemical reaction used to create Cocamidopropyl betaine, was the actual cause of the skin reaction in the patch test. Also a second 6 week study was done on those who had had an allergic reaction from the patch test of the undiluted Cocamidopropyl betaine and they found they had absolutely no allergic reaction when using finished products containing Cocamidopropyl betaine.

A closer look at how patch testing is performed also helps explain why researchers would get a positive result with a patch test of undiluted Cocamidopropyl betaine and a negative result with regular use of a finished product using Cocamidopropyl betaine. Patch testing involves the placement of Cocamidopropyl betaine contained in a small metal cup onto the skin and held against the skin for 48 hours using a paper tape. There is an initial reading done when it is removed after 48 hours and additional readings of the results are done at 72 and 96 hours. Many undiluted ingredients tested this way would cause skin irritation in just about anyone, especially one that is designed to be used in wash off products.

Skin Deep references Haz-Map, Occupational Exposure to Hazardous Agents, which states that Cocamidopropyl betaine is "One of the allergens to which hairdressers may be exposed." This comes from studies showing that Cocamidopropyl betaine in patch tests causes an allergic reaction. The other studies used to back these claims that Cocamidopropyl betaine is an allergen are generally thin to say the least. One study stated that laboratory animals exposed to concentrations exhibited not only swollen eyelids, but also conjunctive irritation and mild to moderate corneal irritation in un-rinsed eyes. I am confident in saying that putting concentrations of almost anything in un-rinsed eyes would cause conjunctive irritation!

Some key factors to keep in mind are that products containing Cocamidopropyl betaine are rinse-off products, and the ingredient is generally formulated into a completed product at low concentrations. Also, as with any ingredient, a small percentage of users are allergic to it, and symptoms of an allergy to Cocamidopropyl betaine are generally mild and include redness, itching or in extreme cases, puffiness.

My vote for this point on the Skin Deep rating system is either give a point for allergen potential to every single ingredient or give it to none of them. There is nothing grown on earth or created in a lab that is not a potential allergen. Given this information, Cocamidopropyl betaine should either have an actual score of 3 or every ingredient should start out with the same 1 point against them.

Ecotoxicology

According to Skin Deep Cocamidopropyl betaine is "suspected to be an environmental toxin" and their reference is the Environmental Canada Domestic Substance List. A thorough search of the Substance List on the official Canadian website, using both trade name Cocamidopropyl betaine and the CAS# 86438-79-1, comes up with this statement, "The substance is not specified on any list" and "there is no control measures imposed on this substance." Another Skin Deep point found to be null and void. So now we are at Cocamidopropyl betaine solidly has a score of 2!

Contamination concerns - Nitrosamines

Cocamidopropyl betaine has an "amine" and "amide" group attached to it. Nitrosamines are produced from nitrites and amines. They can be formed under strongly acidic conditions and high temperatures. Most references to nitrosamines are related to food. Our stomach is a highly acidic condition and fried food can enhance the formation of nitrosamines. Technically speaking what happens is that when food hits the acidic (pH 1.4) condition of the stomach the nitrite forms nitrous acid, which is protonated (addition of a proton to an atom, molecule or ion) and splits into the nitrosonium cation and water which reacts with the amine to produce nitrosamine.

Let's address the pH issue as it relates to cosmetics. Water has a pH of 7 so there isn't a possibility of your shower gel, shampoo, hand soap or cleanser becoming highly acidic when it comes in contact with water. Any personal care product containing Cocamidopropyl betaine most likely has a pH range of 4.5 to 6 because the pH of human skin ranges from 4.5 to 6. Melt and Pour Soaps and true soap have an even higher pH. Amines are nitrosated best in an aqueous solution at pH levels of 3 – 3.4 which your shampoo, shower gel, hand soap, or cleanser have no potential to ever reach.

In relation to the possibility of heat causing nitrosamines in cosmetics most surfactant based formulas require low heat or no heat to manufacture. The chances of the product being heated to 350-375 degrees F (like fried food) are impossible. Also you must keep in mind Cocamidopropyl betaine is generally used in a formula between 5-15%.

Of course all the research regarding nitrosamines causing cancer is related to foods, beer and tobacco and has absolutely nothing what-so-ever to do with rinse-off cosmetics. There is one study that found N-nitrosodimethylamine (NDMA) in drinking water in California which was found to be a by-product of a drinking water treatment. In California the notification level of NDMA is 0.0003 milligrams per liter in drinking water. Cocamidopropyl betaine is absolutely stable and there are no conditions in which it has been or will ever be exposed to, that will cause it to produce nitrosamines.

If you are afraid of the dangers of possible nitrosamine contamination of things from the amine and amide groups, here are a few foods you need to cut out of your diet: beer, fish, dates, kiwifruit, cheese, limes, oranges, passion fruit, tangerine, broccoli, cauliflower, dill pickles, and olives. The foods with high and very high levels need to go first including: avocados, bananas, figs, grapes, lemon, mandarins, pineapples, plums, raspberry, eggplant, mushrooms and tomato, but especially sauerkraut and spinach. Oh wait, I'm not done yet because we still have the Amide group which includes anything with Vitamin B3 and other B vitamins including thiamine, riboflavin, pantothenic acid, pyridoxine, cyanocobalamin, and folic acid. And of course all yeast, meat, fish, milk, eggs, green vegetables, and cereal grains. For more foods you can't eat according to Skin Deep safety ratings see our post about Formaldehyde in response to another false alarm they pulled.

There is absolutely no logical stretch of the imagination that can make this point against Cocamidopropyl betaine legitimate. Give Cocamidopropyl betaine a score of 1 now.

The Last Point
According to Skin Deep Cocamidopropyl betaine is rated as a moderate

hazard due to: Violations, Restrictions & Warning, Allergies/immunotoxicity, Contamination Concerns and Ecotoxicology. We have addressed all of those concerns and vetoed the point given, but that only accounts for 4 points and they rated it a 5. My only guess is that either one of the categories was given extra weight or as Skin Deep says," it adds up the hazards of all ingredients, and is scaled higher if the product has penetration enhancers or other ingredients that increase skin absorption." Since Cocamidopropyl betaine does not contain any penetration enhancers, if that is the reason for the extra point, then the score is 0. If the reason is that one category was given extra weight, the score remains 0 since all points were discredited.

Please un-ring the false alarm pulled by the Environmental Working Groups with their exceptionally flawed Skin Deep rating system.

Addendum II

Scenting Your Soap :: Aromatherapy or Not?

As an Aromatherapist I would be remiss if I didn't address the debate over whether to use fragrance oils or essential oils in your finished soap. The dispute has been going on since 1868 the invention of Coumarin, the first synthetic fragrance. From there the trend towards synthetic fragrances took hold making synthetic scenting economical and aromas consistent. Still today, the positive side of fragrance oils over essential oils is the consistency, cost and variety of non-plant based aromas.

As a Certified and Registered Aromatherapist, I am admittedly biased toward essential oils over fragrance oils. I am also allergic to fragrance oils. Having admitted that up front let me share the debate from the view of an aromatherapist.

The unfortunate side of a synthetic fragrance is the manufactured scent does not contain the therapeutic properties of their counterpart whole-plant based essential oils. Thus, the true power and purpose of aromatherapy is lost. For example, one drop of peppermint fragrance oil does not contain the same natural pharmacy as one drop of the essential oil. The synthetic version only attempts to duplicate the aroma and not the properties transferred from the plant material itself.

Synthetic fragrances have had several other negative issues come to light over the past few years. These include a high rate of allergic reactions as well as the controversy surrounding the undisclosed aroma chemicals and preservatives in every fragrance oil. Many people have chosen to work with fragrance oils because they are intimidated by the powerful properties of essential oils; only to find even fragrance oils often contain minute amounts of essential oils. I'm often asked as an aromatherapist if fragrance oils are safer to use than essential oils because of the potential property effects of essential oils. And the answer is always a resounding no. Fragrance oils are made up of a long list of various chemicals often including essential oils with little regard for the natural qualities that make these oils so precious.

In addition, current laws do not require the full disclosure of the synthetic chemicals making up the fragrance oil. For instance, the formula for green tea fragrance oil contains the chemical compounds in citrus essential oils that cause photosensitization. In addition it contained nutmeg and cinnamon essential oils. Cinnamon essential oil renders the skin hypersensitive to the sun and is a photosensitizing oil. The combination of these two items can be irritating. But since fragrance oil ingredients are not fully disclosed the consumer may be unaware of any potential issues. The crafter using this fragrance oil would not be aware of the presence of cinnamon in the blend when creating their products and may even think that this synthetic fragrance is safer than a natural one.

It is important to know synthetic fragrances work differently on the human body than natural essential oils. The differences between essential and fragrance oils can best be described by a comparison of a real orange to a piece of orange candy. The real orange has health benefits for the body and comes directly from nature. The color, shape, flavor, scent, taste and vitamins, as well as the psychological and physiological benefits, come directly from nature. It was designed to nourish our body as well as provide vitamin C for health benefits. On the other hand, a piece of orange candy gets its sweetness from refined sugar, its shape from gums, it is artificially flavored and colored, has no health benefits whatsoever and can actually be bad for our bodies.

In this example, an essential oil is the orange and a fragrance oil would be the piece of orange candy. The body gains nothing of value from fragrance oil because this man-made substance was only created to duplicate a natural aroma and not the properties. Whereas the essential oil is a function and byproduct of a plant created to protect, heal and pollinate life and is far more beneficial. The hormonal, antimicrobial, antibacterial and, antiviral properties of a plant are captured in the essential oil and enable the human body to use the plants vital energy to benefit itself.

There is no end in sight to the debate over the use of fragrance oils versus essential oils. What is most important is that you as a manufacturer or seller of personal care products, educate yourself on the issue. You should make an informed decision that works with the direction and philosophy of your company. If your marketing campaign is based on aromatherapy and you use synthetic fragrance chemicals to scent, your end product is contrary to your mission statement.

If your market loves strawberry bubble gum, tooty-fruity, or sugar plum and other fun fragrances, know they can only be created synthetically and the aromatherapy marketing would be misleading. Thus the fragrance oil market is the right choice for you and that is okay; both markets have a huge audience. Just keep in mind that consumers are insulted by companies claiming to use aromatherapy while using synthetic fragrance oils that are contrary to their marketing and mission statement. Make it easy for your customers and align your scenting practices with the message of your company. Whether you are a fragrance or essential oil user, the goal is to be true to yourself and your customers.

Glossary of Terms

A

Acid is a compound capable of neutralizing alkalis; anything with a pH lower than 7.

Acidic having a pH lower than 7.

Alcohol(s) is a term used for a large group of organic chemical compounds in which the hydroxyl function group (–OH) is attached to a carbon atom, usually attached to other carbon or hydrogen carbons.

Alkali Salt is a product of the neutralization of a strong base and a weak acid.

Alkaline is a base capable of neutralizing acids; anything with a pH higher than 7.

Amines are organic compounds and functional groups that contain a basic nitrogen atom with a lone pair.

Aminodoamine is a class of chemical compounds used as intermediates in the synthesis of surfactants that are formed from fatty acids and diamines.

Amphoteric surfactants may have either a positive or negative ionic charge. Amphoeteric surfactants adapt to the pH of the water used in the formula. (for example: Cocamidopropyl betaine, Sodium Cocoamphoacetate)

Anionic surfactants have a negative ionic charge. (for example: Sodium Laureth Sulfate, Sodium Lauryl Sulfate, Stearic Acid)

Antioxidants prevent degradation of natural ingredients (proteins, lipids, sugars) in the cosmetics and personal care products. Antioxidants also, protect the skin cells from being damaged by attacking Free Radicals, and slow down the aging process. They have been shown to boost the skin's radiance, minimize age spots, sun spots and fine lines.

Aqueous: of, like or containing water; watery; an aqueous solution.

Aromatherapy simply means "treatment with scent". It is the use essential oils for the treatment of mind and body. The term essential oil comes from the Latin word "essential" which means "essence". Essential oils are volatile because they are able "to fly" since they are a liquid that quickly becomes gaseous. "Aroma" refers to the naturally occurring scent of the essential oils. "Therapy" refers to the physical, psychological, and spiritual treatment imparted from essential oils.

Assay: to test, analyze or evaluate; a substance undergoing analysis; a test.

B

Biodegradable means something is capable of decaying through the action of living organisms; capable of being broken down especially into innocuous products by the action of living things.

Buffering Agent(s) are ingredients that minimize the change in the pH of a solution when an acid or a base is added to the solution.

C

Canadian Hotlist was created by Health Canada to help cosmetic manufacturers satisfy the requirements for sale of a cosmetic. The Hotlist is an administrative list of substances that are restricted and prohibited in cosmetics.

Capric acid is a 10-carbon fatty acid that occurs naturally animal fats, milk and in certain plant oils, including palm and coconut oils.

Caprylic acid is the common name for the 8-carbon saturated fatty acid (also known as octanoic acid) that occurs naturally in the milk of various mammals and is a minor constituent of coconut oil and palm kernel oil.

Carcinogen is a substance that can cause cells to become cancerous by altering their genetic structure so that they multiply continuously and become malignant.

Carotenoids are an organic chemical compound belonging to a group including the carotenes that gives a yellow, orange, or red color to plants.

Cationic surfactants have a positive ionic charge (for example: Cetearyl Alcohol, Stearalkonium Chloride)

Cation is any positively charged atom or group of atoms.

Caustic is a substance capable of burning, corroding, or destroying living tissue.

Caustic soda (also known as lye, sodium hydroxide) is a metallic base used in the manufacturing of soap.

Chemical burns can be caused by acids or bases that come in contact with the skin.

Chemical synthesis is the purposeful execution of chemical reactions to get a new product. A chemical synthesis usually involves the breaking of existing bonds and the formation of new ones.

Choline is a nutrient that helps with brain and memory development. It is an essential nutrient that is required for life's most basic functions, such as normal cell activity, liver function and transporting nutrients throughout the body.

Cleansing Agent(s) are surfactants that clean skin and hair by helping water to mix with oil and dirt so that they can be rinsed away.

Cloud point is the temperature at which a nonionic surfactant starts to become cloudy.

Cosmetic Ingredient Review (CIR) was established in 1976 as an independent safety review program for cosmetic ingredients. The CIR Expert Panel consists of independent experts in dermatology, toxicology, pharmacology and veterinary medicine. The CIR includes participation by the U.S. Food & Drug Administration and the Consumer Federation of America.

Crystalline: having the characteristics or structure of crystals

Cuticle cells are the superficial layer of overlapping cells covering the hair shaft that locks the hair into its follicle.

Cuticle layer is the outermost layer of the hair.

D

D&C is the abbreviation used with colorants for drug and cosmetics. Colors are monitored by the FDA. "Under the Federal Food, Drug, and Cosmetic Act, color additives, except for coal tar hair dyes, are subject to FDA approval before they may be used in food, drugs, or cosmetics, or in medical devices that come in contact with the bodies of people or animals for a significant period of time. The following resources are related to the use of color additives in FDA-regulated products." A colorant with D&C has been approved for use in drugs and cosmetics.

DEG Free Certificate is a certificate to ensure that the glycerin used in cosmetics is not contaminated with diethylene glycol (DEG).

Demulcent is an agent that forms a soothing or protecting film over a mucous membrane.

Denaturant(s) are ingredients that are added to ethyl alcohol (grain alcohol) to make it unsuitable for drinking and create a bitter unappealing taste. Denaturants are controlled by the Alcohol and Tobacco Tax and Trade Bureau in the Department of Treasury in the United States

Depilatory is a cosmetic preparation that removes the unwanted hair from the skin.

Derived: to produce or obtain a compound from another substance by chemical reaction; naturally derived is a substance that can be traced back to natural origins.

Derivative is a substance that is derived from; not original; secondary.

Detergent is a surfactant that acts similar to soap but is not prepared by the saponification of fats and oils.

Diethylene glycol (DEG) is a colorless compound that is poisonous. Chinese manufacturers adulterate glycerin with DEG and caused multiple deaths.

Dissociate (or Dissociation) is the process in which ionic compounds separate for split into smaller particles, ions or radicals.

E

Elasticity of the hair is the measure of how much the hair will stretch and return to its normal state.

Electrolysis is the process by which direct electric current (DC) is passed through a substance to effect a chemical change. The chemical change is one in which the substance loses or gains an electron (oxidation or reduction).

Emollient is a substance used in cosmetics that softens the skin by slowing the evaporation of water.

Emulsifier(s) are ingredients that encourage the suspension of one liquid in another.

Emulsifying Agent(s) in surfactants help to form emulsions by reducing the surface tension of the substances to be emulsified.

Essential oils are highly concentrated and potent oils extracted from plants, trees, seeds, shrubs, flowers, fruit peels and leaves. Essential oils are found in special secretory glands of living plants. The aromatic oils are formed and stored in organs of a plant as a by-product or because of its metabolism.

Esters are chemical compounds derived by reacting an oxoacid with a hydroxyl compound such as an alcohol or phenol.

Esterification reaction is the preparation of an ester.

Exothermic reaction is a chemical reaction that releases energy, usually in the form of heat.

F

Fatty Acid(s) are natural organic compounds that consist of a carboxyl group (oxygen, carbon and hydrogen) attached to a chain of carbon atoms with their associated hydrogen atoms. The chain of carbon atoms may be connected with single bonds, making a 'saturated' fat; or it may contain some double bonds, making an 'unsaturated' fat. The number of carbon and hydrogen atoms in the chain is what determines the qualities of that particular fatty acid. Animal and vegetable fats are made up of various combinations of fatty acids (in sets of three) connected to a glycerol molecule, making them triglycerides.

FD&C means that a color is approved by the FDA for use in Food, Drugs and

Cosmetics. D&C means that a color is approved by the FDA for use in Drugs and Cosmetics.

FD&C Blue No.1 is a dye certified by the FDA as safe for use in Food, Drugs and Cosmetics. It is rated by the World Health Organization as a 1A, completely safe and acceptable for all nonfood use. This color is a U.S. Certified Organic Colorant which means that this colorant is produced in accordance with U.S. Government specifications, and is certified for use in accordance with the Federal Food, Drug and Cosmetic Act.

Foam Booster(s) are surfactants that increase foaming capacity or that stabilize foams.

Free Radical is any atom or molecule that has a single unpaired electron in an outer shell. Free radicals damage the cells, and therefore the cells which form the skin, leads to premature aging and skin wrinkling.

G

Gel phase is the phase in the saponification process in which the soap gets very warm and gelatinous.

General Provisions of the Cosmetics Directive of the European Union includes ingredients other than color additives (Annex IV), preservatives (Annex VI), UV filters (Annex VII), and ingredients not prohibited (Annex II) or restricted (Annex III) that may be used in cosmetic products in the European Union. Ingredients not included in the Annexes of the Cosmetics Directive may be used without restriction, subject to the general principles of protection of human health and good manufacturing practice.

Genotoxic is an agent that is capable of altering the DNA, which causes cancer or mutation.

GRAS is an acronym for the phrase Generally Recognized As Safe. Under sections 201(s) and 409 of the Federal Food, Drug, and Cosmetic Act (the Act), any substance that is intentionally added to food is a food additive, that is subject to premarket review and approval by FDA, unless the substance is generally recognized, among qualified experts, as having been adequately shown to be safe under the conditions of its intended use, or unless the use of the substance is otherwise excluded from the definition of a food additive.

H

Humectant(s) are ingredients that slow the loss of moisture from a product topically applied.

Hygroscopic is to readily take up and retain moisture under conditions of humidity and temperature.

Hydrogenation is a chemical process that adds hydrogen atoms to unsaturated oils.

Hydrolyze is to break down a compound by a chemical reaction with water.

Hydrophilic translates to "water loving" and are substances that are attracted to water.

Hydrotrope(s) are surfactants that have the ability to enhance the water solubility of another surfactant.

Hydroxide ion (Hydroxyl ion) is the anion OH having one oxygen and one hydrogen atom.

Hydroxyl function group is an oxygen-containing group based on an alcohol or OH group.

Hygroscopic is a substance that readily absorbs or attracts moisture from the air.

Hypersensitivity refers to excessive reactions produced by the normal immune system. To have hypersensitivity one must be pre-sensitized to a material.

I

Intermediate in chemistry it is a substance formed as a necessary stage in the manufacture of a desired end product.

Intermittent Mixing is to alternately cease mixing for a time and begin again for a period of time.

Inorganic base is a large class of inorganic compounds, such as Sodium Hydroxide, that neutralize acids.

Intermediate is a short-lived reactive molecule that is produced during the conversion of some reactant to a product.

J

Joint FAO/WHO Expert Committee on Food Additives is an international scientific expert committee that is administered jointly by the Food and Agriculture Organization of the United Nations FAO and the World Health Organization WHO. It has been meeting since 1956, initially to evaluate the safety of food additives. Its work now also includes the evaluation of contaminants, naturally occurring toxicants and residues of veterinary drugs in food.

L

Lauric acid is a saturated fatty acid with a 12-carbon atom chain that occurs in coconut oil.

Lipids are a group of molecules that include fats, oils, waxes, etc., which are lipophilic.

Lipophilic translates to "lipid loving" and are substances that are attracted to lipids.

Long-chain fatty acids are fatty acids with aliphatic tails longer than 12 carbons.

Lot number is an identification numbers that are assigned to a particular lot of materials.

M

Medium-chain fatty acids are fatty acids with aliphatic tails of 6–12 carbons, which can form medium-chain triglycerides.

Medium-chain triglycerides are medium-chain (6 to 12 carbons) fatty acid esters of glycerol.

Melt and Pour Soap Base is a cosmetic base that can be melted down to add color, scent, exfoliants and other additives and then poured into a soap mold to produce a customized soap bar.

Microorganisms are tiny one-celled organisms, viruses, fungi, and bacteria, and are found everywhere in the world.

Miscible means that an ingredient is capable of being mixed with another.

Monographs are a set of rules set by the FDA for Over-the-counter (OTC) drugs which are published in the Federal Register regarding certain ingredients and their intended use.

Monounsaturated fatty acids have a single double bond in the fatty acid chain and all of the remainder of the carbon atoms in the chain is single-bonded.

Mutagenic is a chemical agent that has the ability to change the genetic material of an organism.

Myristic acid is a saturated fatty acid found naturally in nutmeg, palm kernel oil and coconut oil.

N

Neutralize is to make an acidic or alkaline substance chemically neutral.

Nitrosamine(s) is an organic substance formed by a specific reaction of two nitrogen containing substances one of which is an amine, with a second nitrogen containing material (nitrosating agent) such as nitrites used as food preservatives (particularly in lunch meats).

Nonionic surfactants have no charge (for example: Decyl Glucoside, Polysorbate)

Nonvolatile is a substance that does not readily evaporate.

O

Occupational Safety & Health Administration (OSHA) was created by Congress with the Occupational Safety and Health Act of 1970. It is the job of OSHA to ensure safe and healthful working conditions for working men and women by setting and enforcing standards and by providing training, outreach, education and assistance.

Ocular: of or relating to the eye.

Oil-soluble is a substance capable of being dissolved by oil.

Opacifying Agent is a substance that reduces the clear or transparent appearance of cosmetic products.

Organic Compound(s) are compounds that contain carbon and hydrogen and usually other elements such as nitrogen, sulfur and oxygen.

Over-the-counter (OTC) drug is a non-prescription drug regulated by the FDA.

Oxidize to undergo or cause to undergo a chemical reaction with oxygen, as in formation of an oxide.

P

Palmitic acid is a common saturated fatty acid found in palm and coconut oil.

pH Adjuster is an ingredient that is used to control the pH of cosmetic products.

pH is a measurement of the acidity or basicity of a substance. A pH of 7 is considered neutral, a pH lower than 7 is considered acidic, and a pH higher than 7 is considered basic.

Photosensitizer an ingredient or chemical makes a person's skin more sensitive to the ultraviolet light when either ingested, topically or subcutaneously applied.

Poly unsaturated fatty acids is an unsaturated fatty acid with a carbon chain that has more than one double or triple valence bond per molecule.

Polyalcohol is an alcohol that contains more than one hydroxyl group.

Protonate(d): To add a proton to.

Q

QC (Quality Control) is a set process in which materials, processes and manufacturing is reviewed for quality.

R

Raw materials are the basic materials from which products are manufactured.

Reagent is a substance used in a chemical reaction to produce other substances.

Ringworm is a skin infection caused by a fungus.

S

Saponification is the reaction between a caustic alkali (lye) and the fatty acids in a vegetable oil or animal fat that results in soap.

Saturated fat is fat that consists of triglycerides containing only saturated fatty acids.

Sebum is the fatty lubricant matter (your skin's natural oil) secreted by the sebaceous glands of the skin.

Sensitization is an allergic reaction to a particular irritant; in sensitization studies the skin becomes increasingly reactive to the substance as a result of subsequent exposures.

Short-chain fatty acids are fatty acids with aliphatic tails of fewer than six carbons.

Skin conditioning agents are ingredients that act as lubricants on the skin surface, which give the skin a soft and smooth appearance.

Sodium chloride is a white crystalline solid commonly known as table salt.

Solubilize: to make a substance soluble or more soluble.

Solubilizing Agent are substances that help another ingredient to dissolve in a solvent in which it would not normally dissolve.

Soluble: able to dissolve.

Solvent: a substance that dissolves another substance.

Standard Operating Procedures (SOP) is a written set of instruction that details all steps of a manufacturing process that could affect the quality of the product.

Subchronic study is a repeat dose study that usually ranges from a period of days to months that involves exposure to a substance for 10% of the lifespan of a species lifetime.

Surface active agent: See Surfactant

Surfactant(s) are a vehicle used in cosmetic chemistry. They are important building blocks in personal care products. Surfactants allow cosmetics to slip across, onto or to clean the skin by breaking up and separating from the skin, oils, fats, makeup, dirt, pollution and other debris.

There are four basic types of surfactants used in cosmetics. 1. Anionic surfactants have a negative ionic charge. 2. Cationic surfactants have a positive ionic charge. Amphoteric surfactants may have either a positive or negative ionic charge. 3. Amphoeteric surfactants adapt to the pH of the water used in the formula. 4. Nonionic surfactants have no charge.

Surfactants by definition lower the surface tension of the skin and/or of the water in a formula. Surfactants are both hydrophilic (water loving) and lipophilic (oil loving) which gives them the ability to reduce surface tension in a water and oil formula. Surfactants are commonly used in products that are designed to cleanse (shampoo, shower gel, face cleanser, hand soap), emulsify water and oil (lotion, crème), solubilize (polysorbate solubizing essential oil into a toner, body mist) or condition (hair conditioner). Surfactants are also known as Surface Active Agents.

Synthesis is the forming or building of a more complex substance or compound from elements or simpler compounds.

T

Teratogenic is a substance that is able to disturb the growth and development of an embryo or fetus.

Thickening agents are added to cosmetics to change the consistency.

Toxicity is the degree to which a substance can harm animals or humans.

Triglyceride is an ester derived from glycerol and three fatty acids. It is the main constituent of vegetable oil and animal fats.

U

United States Pharmacopeia (USP) is a non–governmental, official public standards–setting authority for prescription and over–the–counter medicines and other healthcare products manufactured or sold in the United States. USP also sets widely recognized standards for food ingredients and dietary supplements. USP sets standards for the quality, purity, strength, and consistency of these products–critical to the public health.

V

Viscosity is a measure of the resistance of a fluid to deformation under shear stress. It is commonly perceived as "thickness", or resistance to pouring.

W

Water-soluble: able to dissolve in water.

Business and Regulatory Resources

A

A Consumer's Dictionary of Cosmetic Ingredients
Complete Information About the Harmful and Desirable Ingredients Found in Cosmetics and Cosmeceuticals by Ruth Winter, M.S.

All Business Resource
http://www.allbusiness.com/
All Business, A D&B Company
650 Townsend Street, Suite 450
San Francisco, CA 94103
Telephone: 415-694-5000
Fax: 415-694-50001

Alliance of International Aromatherapists
http://www.alliance-aromatherapists.org/
Alliance of International Aromatherapists
Suite 323
9965 W. Remington Place – Unit A10
Littleton, Colorado 80128
E-mail: info@alliance-aromatherapists.org
Telephone: 303-531-6377
Toll Free: 1-877-531-6377
Fax: 303-979-7135

American Cancer Society
http://www.cancer.org
Telephone: 1-800-227-2345 (or 1-866-228-4327 for TTY)

American Botanical Council (ABC)
http://abc.herbalgram.org
 American Botanical Council
6200 Manor Rd.
Austin, TX 78723
E-mail: abc@herbalgram.org
Telephone: 512-926-4900
Fax: 512-926-2345

American Council on Truth and Science
http://www.acsh.org/
American Council on Science and Health
1995 Broadway, Second Floor
New York, NY 10023-5860
E-mail: acsh@acsh.org
Telephone: 212-362-7044

Toll free: 866-905-2694
Fax: 212-362-4919

American Herbal Products Association
http://www.ahpa.org/
American Herbal Products Association
8630 Fenton Street, Suite 918
Silver Spring, MD 20910
E-mail: ahpa@ahpa.org
Telephone: 301-588-1171
Fax: 301-588-1174

Aromatherapy Registration Council
http://www.aromatherapycouncil.org/
Aromatherapy Registration Council
C/- 5940 SW Hood Ave.
Portland, OR 97039
E-mail: info@aromatherapycouncil.org
Telephone: 503-244-0726
Fax: 503-244-0727

Aromatherapy Supplies
Essential Wholesale & Labs
2211 NW Nicolai St.
Portland, OR 97210
Telephone: 503-722-7557
www.essentialwholesale.com

B

Better Business Bureau
http://www.bbb.org/online/
The Council of Better Business Bureaus
4200 Wilson Blvd., Suite 800
Arlington, VA 22203-1838

C

California Safe Cosmetics Program
http://www.cdph.ca.gov/programs/cosmetics/
Pages/default.aspx
Telephone: 916-558-1784

Canadian Council of Better Business Bureaus
2 St. Clair Ave. East
Toronto, ON M4T 2T5
Telephone: 703-276-0100
Fax: 703-525-8277

Canadian Cosmetic, Toiletry and Fragrance Association (CCTFA),
http://www.cctfa.ca/site/cctfa/
Canadian Cosmetic, Toiletry and Fragrance Association
420 Britannia Road East, Suite 102
Mississauga, Ontario
L4Z 3L5
E-mail: cctfa@cctfa.ca
Telephone: 905-890-5161
Fax: 905-890-2607

Contract Manufacturing/Packaging
Essential Wholesale & Labs
2211 NW Nicolai St.
Portland, OR 97210
Telephone: 503-905-3273
www.essentialwholesale.com

Cosmetic Ingredient Review Panel
http://www.cir-safety.org/
Cosmetic Ingredient Review
1101 17th St. N.W., Suite 412
Washington D.C. 20036-4702
E-mail: cirinfo@cir-safety.org
Telephone: 202-331-0651
Fax: 202-331-0088

Cosmetic Bench Reference
http://dir.cosmeticsandtoiletries.com
Allured Business Media
336 Gundersen Drive, Suite A
Carol Stream, IL 60188-2403
E-mail: cbr@allured.com
Telephone: 1-630-653-2155
Fax: 1-630-653-2192

Cosmetics Info
http://www.cosmeticsinfo.org/

Cosmetics Toiletry and Perfume Association
http://dir.cosmeticsandtoiletries.com
Allured Business Media
336 Gundersen Drive, Suite A
Carol Stream, IL 60188-2403
E-mail: cbr@allured.com
Telephone: 1-630-653-2155
Fax: 1-630-653-2192

D

Disaster Information Management Research Center (DIMRC)
One Democracy Plaza, Suite 1030
6701 Democracy Blvd., MSC 4876
Bethesda, MD 20892

E

Environmental Health and Toxicity
http://sis.nlm.nih.gov/enviro.html
Specialized Information Services (SIS)
Two Democracy Plaza, Suite 510
6707 Democracy Blvd., MSC 5467
Bethesda, MD 20892-5467
E-mail: tehip@teh.nlm.nih.gov
Telephone: 301-496-1131 (local and int'l)
Toll Free: 1-888-FINDNLM
Fax: 1-301-480-3537

Essential U Blog
http://www.essentialublog.com/blog

Etsy
http://www.etsy.com/
Set up your store under "Bath & Beauty"

European Commission CosIng
http://ec.europa.eu/consumers/cosmetics/cosing/
European Commission
Health & Consumers Directorate-General
B – 1049 Brussels
Belgium

eWomen Network
http://www.ewomennetwork.com
eWomenNetwork, Inc.
14900 Landmark Blvd., Suite 540
Dallas, TX 75254
E-mail: info@ewomennetwork.com
Telephone: 972-620-9995
Fax: 972-720-9995

F

Food and Drug Administration (FDA)
http://www.fda.gov/Cosmetics/default.htm
Food and Drug Administration
10903 New Hampshire Ave.
Silver Spring, MD 20993-0002
Telephone: 888-463-6332, 301-796-8240, or 866-300-4374 (Emergency Operations)

Fragrance Materials Association of the United States
http://www.fmafragrance.org/
International Fragrance Association North America
1620 Street NW, Suite 925
Washington D.C. 20006
E-mail: info@ifrana.org
Telephone: 202-293-5800
Fax: 202-463-8998

Free Conference Calling
http://www.freeconferencecalling.com/

Free Small Business Help
http://www.buzgate.org/index.html
Buzgate.org
c/o P.O. Box 219
E. Kingston, NH 03827

H

Handcrafted Soapmakers Guild
http://www.soapguild.org/
Handcrafted Soapmakers Guild
P.O. Box 5103
Portland, OR 97208-5103
E-mail: info@soapguild.org
Telephone: 1-866-900-SOAP (866-900-7627)
or 503-283-7758
Fax: 503-286-0236

Health Canada
http://www.hc-sc.gc.ca/cps-spc/index-eng.php
Health Canada
Address Locator 0900C2
Ottawa, Ontario
KIA OK9
E-mail: Info@hc-sc.gc.ca
Telephone: 613-957-2991
Toll free: 1-866-225-0709
Facsimile: 613-941-5366
Teletypewriter: 1-800-267-1245 (Health Canada)

Household Products Data Base
http://hpd.nlm.nih.gov/index.htm
U.S. National Library of Medicine
8600 Rockville Pike
Bethesda, MD 20894
E-mail: tehip@teh.nlm.nih.gov

How to Follow the Rules and Regs Explained in Plain English by Marie Gale
http://www.mariegale.com/purchase-soap-cosmetic-labeling-book/

I

INCI Dictionary
http://www.essentiallabs.com/PDF/INCI_NAMES_3col.pdf

Independent Cosmetic Manufacturers and Distributors (ICMAD)
http://www.icmad.org/
Independent Cosmetic Manufacturers and Distributors
1220 W. Northwest Hwy
Palatine, IL 60067
E-mail: info@icmad.org
Toll Free: 800-334-2623
Fax: 847-991-8161

Indie Beauty Network
http://www.indiebeauty.com
E-mail: indiebusiness@gmail.com
Telephone: 704-291-7280
Send an email to request the mailing address

International Federation of Aromatherapist
http://www.ifaroma.org/
International Federation of Aromatherapist, UK Head Office
7B Walpole Court
Ealing Green
Ealing, London
W5 5ED
Telephone: 020 8567 2243 or 020 8567 1923
Fax: 020 8840 9288

International Fragrance Association
http://www.ifraorg.org/
IFRA Operations
Avenue des Arts, 6 1210
Brussels Belgium
IFRA Head Office
Chemin de la Parfumerie 5CH-1214
Vernier, Geneva Switzerland
IFRA Operations
Telephone: +32-2214 20 60
Fax: +32-2 214 2069
IFRA Head Office
Telephone: +41-22 431 82 50
Fax: +41-22 431 88 06

IRS Small Business and Self-Employed Tax Center
http://www.irs.gov/businesses/small/index.html

J

Just Sell Resources
http://www.justsell.com/
Give more Media, Inc.
2500 Gaskins Rd.
Richmond, VA 23238
E-mail: sparker@givemore.com
Telephone: 804-762-4500 ext. 303

L

Ladies Who Launch
http://www.ladieswholaunch.com/
Ladies Who Launch, Inc.
46 Shopping Plaza #190
Chagrin Falls, OH 44022
E-mail: info@ladieswholaunch.com
Telephone: 440-247-2239

N

National Association for the Self-Employed
http://nase.org/Home.aspx
National Association for the Self-Employed
P.O. Box 241
Annapolis Junction, MD 20701-0241
Toll Free: 1-800-649-6273 (Continental US)
or 1-800-232-6273 (Alaska and Hawaii)

Natural Association of Holistic Aromatherapists
http://www.naha.org/
Natural Association of Holistic Aromatherapists
P.O. Box 1868
Banner Elk, NC 28604
E-mail: info@naha.org
Telephone: 828-898-6161
Fax: 828-898-1965

National Association of Women Business Owners
http://nawbo.org/
NAWBO
601 Pennsylvania Ave. NW
South Building, Suite 900
Washington, DC 20004
E-mail: national@nawbo.org

Toll Free: 800-55-NAWBO (800-556-2926)
Fax: 202-403-3788

National Federation of Independent Business
http://www.nfib.com/
National Federation of Independent Business
53 Century Blvd. – Suite 250
Nashville, TN 37214
Telephone: 615-872-5800
Toll Free: 800-634-2669

O

Occupational Safety & Health Administration
http://www.osha.gov/
U.S. Department of Labor
Occupational Safety & Health Administration
200 Constitution Avenue
Washington, D.C. 20210
1-800-321-6742

Organic Consumers Association
http://www.organicconsumers.org/
Organic Consumers Association
6771 South Silver Hill Drive
Finland, MN 55603
Telephone: 218-226-4164
Fax: 218-353-7652

P

Personal Care Products Council
http://www.ctfa.org/
The Personal Care Products Council
1101 17th Street NW, Suite 300
Washington D.C. 20036-4702
Telephone: 202-331-1770
Fax: 202-331-1969

Personal Care Truth
http://personalcaretruth.com/

Press Release Info
http://toolkit.prnewswire.com/score/index.shtml#

Private Label Cosmetics
Essential Wholesale & Labs
2211 NW Nicolai St.
Portland, OR 97210
Telephone: 503-905-3273
www.essentialwholesale.com

Pub Med
http://www.ncbi.nlm.nih.gov/sites/entrez

National Center of Biotechnology Information
National Library of Medicine
8600 Rockville Pike, Building 38A
Bethesda, MD 20894
E-mail: info@ncbi.nlm.nih.gov
Telephone: 301-496-2475

S

SCORE
http://www.score.org/index.html
Toll Free: 800-634-0245

Sense About Science
http://www.senseaboutscience.org.uk
Sense About Science
25 Shaftesbury Avenue
London W1D 7ET
E-mail: enquiries@senseaboutscience.org
Telephone: +44 (0)20 7478 4380

Small Business Loan Sources
http://www.ibank.com/

Soap Making Supplies
Essential Wholesale & Labs
2211 NW Nicolai St.
Portland, OR 97210
www.essentialwholesale.com
Telephone: 503-722-7557

Social Security Online
http://www.socialsecurity.gov/employer/
Toll Free: 800-772-1213 or 1-800-325-0778 (TTY)
Social Security Administration
Office of Public Inquires
Windsor Park Building
6401 Security Blvd.
Baltimore, MD 21235

Society of Cosmetic Chemists
http://www.scconline.org/website/index.shtml
Society of Cosmetic Chemists
120 Wall Street, Suite 2400
New York, NY 10005-4088
E-mail: scc@scconline.org
Telephone: 212-668-1500
Fax: 212-668-1504

Society of Cosmetic Scientists
http://www.scs.org.uk/
SCS / IFSCC
Suite 6
Langham House East
Mill Street
LUTON
Bedfordshire LU1 2NA, UK
E-mail: lorna.weston@ifscc.org (Lorna Weston, Secretary General, IFSCC), gem.bektas@btconnect.com (Gem Bektas, Secretary General, SCS), or mel.cheekoory@btconnect.com (Mel Cheekoory, Admin. Assistant)
Telephone: 01582 726661
Fax: 01582 405217

Start a Business Today
http://www.bizfilings.com/default.aspx
BizFilings
8040 Excelsior Dr., Suite 200
Madison, WI 53717
Telephone: 608-827-5300
Toll Free: 800-981-7183

Stats
http://stats.org/index.htm
Statistical Assessment Service
2100 L. Street, Suite 300
Washington D.C. 20037
Telephone: 202-223-2942
Fax: 202-872-4014

T

ToxNet
http://toxnet.nlm.nih.gov/index.html
Specialized Information Services (SIS)
Two Democracy Plaza, Suite 510
6707 Democracy Blvd., MSC 5467
Bethesda, MD 20892-5467
E-mail: tehip@teh.nlm.nih.gov
Telephone: 301-496-1131 (local and international)
Toll Free: 1-888-FINDNLM
Fax (SIS): 1-301-480-3537
Fax (DIMRC): 1-301-480-9680

U

US Association for Small Business and Entrepreneurship
http://usasbe.org/
USASBE
Belmont University
1900 Belmont Blvd.
Nashville, TN 37212
E-mail: usasbe@belmont.edu
Telephone: +1-615-460-2615
Fax: +1-615-460-2614

US Chamber of Commerce
http://www.uschamber.com/
U.S. Chamber of Commerce
1615 H Street, NW
Washington DC, 20062-2000
Telephone: 202-659-6000
Toll Free: 800-638-6582

US Consumer Product Safety Commission
http://www.cpsc.gov/
U.S. Consumer Product Safety Commission
4330 East West Highway
Bethesda, MD 20814
Telephone: 301-504-7923
Toll free: 800-638-2772
Fax: 301-504-0124 and 301-504-0025

US Department of Commerce
http://www.commerce.gov/
U.S. Department of Commerce
1401 Constitution Avenue, NW
Washington, DC 20230
E-mail: TheSec@doc.gov (Secretary Locke)
Telephone: 202-482-2000

US Small Business Administration
http://www.sba.gov/
US Small Business Administration
409 3rd Street, SW
Washington, DC 20416
E-mail: answerdesk@sba.gov
Telephone: 704-344-6640 (TTY)
Toll Free: 800-827-5722

Equipment and Suppliers

Certified Lye
www.certified-lye.com

Essential Wholesale & Labs
2211 NW Nicolai St.
Portland, OR 97210
Supplies for the recipes in this book can be found online at
www.essentialwholesale.com
Telephone: 503-722-7557

Indco Mixers
http://www.indco.com/

Jiffy Mixer Co, Inc
http://www.jiffymixer.com/

Marie Gale
How to Follow the Rules and Regs Explained in Plain English by Marie Gale.
http://www.mariegale.com/purchase-soap-cosmetic-labeling-book

Milky Way Molds
http://www.milkywaymolds.com/

Shoot Y'all Photography
http://shootyallphotography.com
info@shootyallphotography.com

Soap Equipment
www.soapequipment.com

Soap Molds.com
2138 Humboldt St
Bellingham, WA 98226
Telephone: 360-671-0201
http://www.soapmolds.com/

You can find a complete list of Packaging Suppliers here:
http://www.essentialwholesale.com/Packaging-Resources

References

Fowler, J. F., Fowler, L. M. and Hunter, J. E. (1997), Allergy to cocamidopropyl betaine may be due to amidoamine: a patch test and product use test study. Contact Dermatitis, 37: 276–281. doi: 10.1111/j.1600-0536.1997.tb02464.x

California Department of Public Health, NDMA and Other Nitrosamines - Drinking Water Issues, http://www.cdph.ca.gov/certlic/drinkingwater/Pages/NDMA.aspx

Castor Oil, USP: MSDS; http://www.essentialwholesale.com/Learning-Library/MSDS

Cocamidopropyl betaine: MSDS; Certificate of Analysis; Product Bulletin; Mammalian Toxicity Report; Biodegradability Report; http://www.essentialwholesale.com/Learning-Library/MSDS

Coconut Oil: MSDS; http://www.essentialwholesale.com/Learning-Library/MSDS

Cosmetic Ingredient Review, CIR Annual Report, CIR Compendium, CIR Ingredient Reports, http://www.cir-safety.org/publications.shtml

Cosmetic Ingredient Review, Quick Reference Table, Cosmetics Ingredient Reports through June 2010, http://www.cir-safety.org/staff_files/PublicationsListDec2009.pdf

Denatured Alcohol: MSDS, http://www.essentialwholesale.com/Learning-Library/MSDS

European Commission, Health and Consumers, Cosmetics-CosIng, http://ec.europa.eu/consumers/cosmetics/cosing/

European Commission, Health and Consumers, Cosmetics-CosIng, Annexes, http://ec.europa.eu/consumers/cosmetics/cosing/index.cfm?fuseaction=ref_data.annexes_v2

European Commission, Health and Consumers, Cosmetics-CosIng, Regulations and Directives, http://ec.europa.eu/consumers/cosmetics/cosing/index.cfm?fuseaction=ref_data.regulations

FDA, U.S. Food and Drug Administration, Cosmetics, http://www.fda.gov/Cosmetics/default.htm

FDA, U.S. Food and Drug Administration, Cosmetics Labeling & Label Claims, http://www.fda.gov/Cosmetics/CosmeticLabelingLabelClaims/default.htm

FDA, U.S. Food and Drug Administration, Federal Food, Drug, and Cosmetics Act (FD&C Act), http://www.fda.gov/RegulatoryInformation/Legislation/FederalFoodDrugandCosmeticActFDCAct/default.htm

FDA, U.S. Food and Drug Administration, Good Manufacturing Practice (GMP) Guildelines/Inspections Checklist, http://www.fda.gov/Cosmetics/GuidanceComplianceRegulatoryInformation/GoodManufacturingPracticeGMPGuidelinesInspectionChecklist/default.htm

FDA, U.S. Food and Drug Administration, Guidance, Compliance & Regulatory Information, http://www.fda.gov/Cosmetics/GuidanceComplianceRegulatoryInformation/default.htm

FDA, U.S. Food and Drug Administration, Is It a Cosmetic, a Drug, or Both? (Or Is It Soap?), http://www.fda.gov/Cosmetics/GuidanceComplianceRegulatoryInformation/ucm074201.htm

FDA, U.S. Food and Drug Administration, Product and Ingredient Safety, http://www.fda.gov/Cosmetics/ProductandIngredientSafety/default.htm

Glycerin: MSDS; http://www.essentialwholesale.com/Learning-Library/MSDS

Health Canada, List of Prohibited and Restricted Cosmetic Ingredients ("Hotlist"), http://www.hc-sc.gc.ca/cps-spc/cosmet-person/indust/hot-list-critique/index-eng.php

Health Canada, Cosmetics and Your Health, http://www.hc-sc.gc.ca/hl-vs/iyh-vsv/prod/cosmet-eng.php

Health Canada, Consumer Product Safety, http://www.hc-sc.gc.ca/cps-spc/cosmet-person/indust/index-eng.php

Health Canada, Cosmetics and Personal Care, For Consumers and For Industry and Professionals, http://www.hc-sc.gc.ca/cps-spc/cosmet-person/index-eng.php

Japan Ministry of Health, Labor and Welfare, Standards for Cosmetics, No. 331 of 2000, http://www.mhlw.go.jp/english/dl/cosmetics.pdf

Lauramide DEA: MSDS; Certificate of Analysis; Product Bulletin; Mammalian Toxicity Report; Biodegradability Report; http://www.essentialwholesale.com/Learning-Library/MSDS

Merriam-Webster Online Dictionary, 2011 Merriam-Webster, Incorporated, http://www.merriam-webster.com

Myristic Acid: MSDS; Certificate of Analysis; Product Bulletin; Mammalian Toxicity Report; Biodegradability Report; http://www.essentialwholesale.com/Learning-Library/MSDS

National Toxicity Program, Department of Health and Human Services; http://ntp.niehs.nih.gov/

Occupational Safety & Health Administration, Regulations (Standards – 29 CFR), http://www.osha.gov/

Propylene Glycol: MSDS; Certificate of Analysis; Product Bulletin; Mammalian Toxicity Report; Biodegradability Report; http://www.essentialwholesale.com/Learning-Library/MSDS

PubMed.gov, U.S. National library of Medicine, National Institute of Health, http://www.ncbi.nlm.nih.gov/pubmed/

Regulatory Toxicology and Pharmacology, Official Journal of the International Society for Regulatory Toxicology and Pharmacology, Elsevier Science, Gio B. Gori, DSc, MPH, ATS

Science Dictionary, Chemistry Terms and Definitions Listed Alphabetically, Science Dictionary - Scientific Definitions 2003-2006, http://www.sciencedictionary.org/chemistry/

Sodium C14-16 Olefin Sulfonate: MSDS; Certificate of Analysis; Product Bulletin;

Mammalian Toxicity Report; Biodegradability Report; http://www.essentialwholesale.com/Learning-Library/MSDS

Sodium Hydroxide: MSDS; Certificate of Analysis; Product Bulletin; Mammalian Toxicity Report; Biodegradability Report; http://www.essentialwholesale.com/Learning-Library/MSDS

Sodium Laureth Sulfate: MSDS; Certificate of Analysis; Product Bulletin; Mammalian Toxicity Report; Biodegradability Report; http://www.essentialwholesale.com/Learning-Library/MSDS

Sorbitol: MSDS; http://www.essentialwholesale.com/Learning-Library/MSDS

Stearic Acid: MSDS; Certificate of Analysis; Product Bulletin; Mammalian Toxicity Report; Biodegradability Report; http://www.essentialwholesale.com/Learning-Library/MSDS

The Center for Drug Evaluation and Research (CDER), http://www.fda.gov/Drugs/default.htm

Titanium Dioxide: MSDS; http://www.essentialwholesale.com/Learning-Library/MSDS

Triethanolamine: MSDS; Certificate of Analysis; Product Bulletin; Mammalian Toxicity Report; Biodegradability Report; http://www.essentialwholesale.com/Learning-Library/MSDS

U.S. Consumer Product Safety Commission, Office of Compliance, Requirements under the Federal Hazardous Substances Act: Labeling and Banning Requirements for Chemical and Other Hazardous Substances, 15 U.S.C, 161 and 16 C.F.R. Part 1500, http://www.cpsc.gov/BUSINFO/regsumfhsa.pdf

U.S. Consumer Product Safety Commission, Office of Compliance, Requirements under the Poison Prevention Packaging Act, 16 C.F.R. 1700, http://www.cpsc.gov/BUSINFO/regsumpppa.pdf

Coming Soon!

An Intermediate Guide to Melt & Pour Soap Base Manufacturing
and
The Business & Science of Aromatherapy

Index

G

Gel phase 73
Genotoxic 18-19
Gloves 11, 18, 26, 56, 60
GMP 11, 30, 33, 35, 37, 39, 42, 49-50, 56-70
Goggles 11, 26
GRAS 15, 17-18, 20-21

H

Hair conditioner 4-5
Hazardous Material 24, 25
Humectant 12, 14, 20
Hydrolyze 16, 18
Hydrophilic 14
Hygroscopic 22

I

Inorganic base 18
Iron Oxide 44-45

L

Labeling 2, 25, 47, 49-50, 53-54, 60, 63, 65, 67, 69
Laboratory Controls 66, 68
Lather 14, 17, 20
Lauramide DEA 12, 15-16, 32, 38, 41, 43
Lauric acid 14, 16-17
Leave-on Products 13, 19, 76
Lipids 5, 48
Lipophilic 14
Lot number 63, 65-67, 70
Lye 10-11, 18, 24-39, 42, 58, 72-73

M

Mask 11, 18, 26
Mica 44-45
Misbranded 49-50, 56
Miscible 14, 17
MSDS 19, 24-25, 27
Mutagenic 13, 16
Myristic Acid 14, 16, 1, 31-42, 75

N

"Natural" Melt & Pour Soap 72-75
Neutralize 11, 22, 28
Nitrosamines 22, 78-79
Nonvolatile 48

O

Oil-soluble 22
Opacifying Agent 16
Oxidize 14

P

Palm Oil 16-17, 72, 74
Personnel 25, 58, 60
pH 5, 13, 18, 22, 28, 66-67, 78-79
Product Claims 52
Production 2, 57, 63, 65, 67-68
Propylene Glycol 17-18, 30-39, 41-44, 74-75

Q

QC (Quality Control) 60, 62-67

R

S

T

V

W

30572470R00067

Made in the USA
Lexington, KY
08 March 2014